The Amazing True Story of

Abba Child Care

Cover design by: Remco de Vries, route5.nl

ISBN: 978-1-964794-82-2   1 2 3 4 5 6 7 8 9 10

Printed in the United States of America

WHAT PEOPLE ARE SAYING ABOUT
Abba Child Care

As I read this book, I was deeply moved at how faithful God has been and how He has worked to connect Jaap and me for His divine mission. The book is a powerful reminder of His guidance and presence on our life journey. I had an emotional rollercoaster experience reading all the stories. There were so many ups and downs on that rollercoaster, so much joy and so many tears, so much fear and so much faith. Through it all, God has been faithful and gracious. To see our journey recorded in a book is another miracle. Thank you so much, Jaap, for the painstaking efforts to record all the details of the past two decades and bring them to light again. To the readers: As you read, be inspired and encouraged by God's goodness, grace, and provision. Highly recommend.

—Kingsly Lazarus
Abba, India

This book shows you how God is the director of our lives and provider through His work. Kingsly and Jaap are two faithful men of God, determined and dedicated to preaching the good news and caring for orphans and widows. It is very clear that God has attached His blessing to their work. Personally, I am very impressed by the fearlessness with which our brothers in India share the love of Christ in a raw, direct, passionate, and yet tender way. I thank God that for years, I have been able to sow in and be involved in this beautiful and fruitful work of our God.

—Chris Koelewijn
Friend and board member of Abba and Heilbode

In this beautiful book, Jaap Dieleman invites and inspires us to immerse ourselves in the remarkable stories of over twenty years of mission work in India. The journey God sent Jaap and Kingsly on is inconceivable, one that neither of them could have ever imagined when they met some twenty years ago. In retrospect, it is clear that God truly is the author of this amazing story. Now, we can all experience joy and blessing through this wonderful story of Abba. A must-read for everyone!

—Anonymous friend

Jaap Dieleman says he is held together by grace, but to me, he is a hero of faith. Courageous, faithful to the Bible, and led by the Spirit, he has a faith and perseverance that inspires me. The fruit of his ministry can only be explained by God's work, which we—even to the best of our abilities—cannot change or control. In Abba Child Care's work, we see how caring for widows and orphans and preaching the good news go together, followed by mighty miracles and signs. I would say, "We do the possible, and God does the impossible!" I long for this kind of faith. That is why this book, full of wonderful guidance from God, is an absolute must for today, because it does not tell us what we can do but what God can do!

—Hans Maat
Return of Hope & European Mission Center

Wow—wonder and emotion fill this book—a remarkable account of a God-initiated encounter and ministry: Abba Child Care. In a 1994 address, Mother Teresa said, "The greatest gift that God has given us is to fight abortion with adoption." The compassion and care that Kingsly and Jaap have invested in the care of orphans and widows are incredible. The resulting gospel projects in India are fantastic extensions and evidence of God's guidance and provision. His mighty hand is evident throughout Jaap's story. This reading is immensely enjoyable!

—John Howard
Former Editor-in-Chief, Charisma Magazine

One miracle is special, but a story of one miracle followed by another is exceptional. The story of Abba Child Care was surely authored by God Himself. It is the true story of Jaap Dieleman and Kingsley Lazarus, who were brought together, and, in faith and humility, embarked on an unforgettable adventure with God. What started with the miracle of a child raised from the dead in the womb has now grown into a miracle that has changed the course of India forever and continues to change to the honor and glory of Jesus Christ.

—Daniel Dieleman
Board member Abba Child Care

This is not a textbook. It is a history book—but not like those school-books filled with boring dates and long lists of impressive events: wars, naval battles, migrations, etc. This history book is a brilliant account of the life of Abba Child Care, the Christian aid organization in India founded by Jaap and Kingsly. The book is a first-hand account of the events that sparked the genesis of Abba and grew to its present-day mission. There are reports of "wars," but they are not military wars; they are spiritual and all won with the help of God. Jaap and Kingsly witnessed fantastic victories over the realm of demonic cultural traditions that have overcome issues like poverty in India through the unfailing love of God's children. This book is too small to contain all the successes that took place!

—Dick van Bloois

This book really is a must-read because it is full of faith adventures! Jaap Dieleman's stories will amaze you as evidence of the greatness of God. Nothing will elevate your faith more than learning about the faith adventures of others—that is why the Bible is full of stories of ordinary people whom Almighty God used in a special way. Read Jaap's story and be inspired!

—Tom de Wal
Frontrunners

It is wonderful and incomprehensible how God, the great Director, carries out His script in the fabric of our lives. It is impressive how He brings people together, uses situations, and places them on His timeline. It is amazing how He gives us inspiration to fulfill His purposes. As an eyewitness and traveling companion of just a small part of this story, I was privileged to experience God's great and indescribable love. This book gives a heartwarming and encouraging reminder about how God makes great things happen through fatherly hearts and the courage of two men. To HIM, all thanks and honor.

—Mattanja in 't Veld
Friend and traveling companion

I am amazed by everything in this book and was reminded of Nehemiah 6:16, which states that everyone (including the enemy) had to acknowledge that the rebuilding of the city wall in such a short period of time (fifty-two days!) was accomplished only by God's help. This book is full of miracles and mysteries, just like the Bible—Peter walks out of prison the first time. Such things happen in this book, too—miraculous help and deliverances, but also a certain 'Daniel' who is murdered. But in all this, we clearly see the hand of God in the salvation of those thousands of souls. Many blessings when reading and translating it into your own life!

—Anton Doornenbal

The Amazing True Story of

Abba Child Care

Jaap Dieleman

FO UR

I dedicate this book to all of you who have faithfully supported and given your lives to our vision all these years with your prayers and support to make our dream a reality: preachers, evangelists, volunteers, laborers, workers in the field, and dear friends. Your sacrifices have not been in vain, and we hope those of you who don't see the fulfillment of this dream happen in your lifetime will one day see its fulfillment in heaven.

CONTENTS

ABOUT THE BOOK

This book tells the true story of Abba Child Care—an amazing story of divine encounters, deep friendships, pure passion, painful experiences, astonishing miracles, supernatural provision, unspeakable joy, and God's eternal love. It is the story of two friends, Kingsly Lazarus and me, Jaap Dieleman, who were mysteriously brought together by God, to the glory of His plan for our lives. Both Kingsly and I give all the glory to God for the great things He has done and know that without each other, we could not have accomplished all that we have.

More importantly, we are fully aware that none of this would have been possible without God. All honor and glory belong to Almighty God, who has guided us. The story is still ongoing, even as I write this book, and only God knows where it will lead. We warmly welcome you to come aboard and experience this adventure with us. We wish you a blessed journey!

To protect the identity of certain people, we have given them pseudonyms. Any resemblance to real persons is purely coincidental.

A WORD OF THANKS

I would like to take this opportunity to thank everyone who has been involved in Abba's work from the very beginning.

To Aart de Landmeter who designed Abba's logo for us.

To Ulfert and Wichard, who were the first to travel to India with me and were at the cradle of the Abba Children's Home.

And to Ben, Ulfert, and Daniel, who were the first to take a seat on the board of the foundation.

I am also incredibly grateful for the many small and large sponsors who have supported a child and/or a widow for many years.

Others have donated a sewing machine, sponsored a medical camp, supported a pastor or teacher, or donated a pair of orthopedic shoes to the lepers. Many have donated a multifunctional village hall or a gospel truck that we use to win many precious souls. I cannot possibly mention everyone, but I am so grateful for the many nameless people who have supported our work from their hearts.

I want to thank my current Dutch team: Chris, Ronald, and Daniel, who help with manual labor and other services.

xvi Abba Child Care

Thank you to our special sponsors—Mark, John, Jan, Janny, Jo, Arjen, Tom, Lydia, Huub, Ronald, Bart, and many others—who have done so much to make the impossible possible. Thank you all.

Thank you, Remco. You have shaped our work over the years through magazines and other publications.

Dick, with his talent for language, cleaned up my writings into readable work (like this book, by the way!)

Thank you to my dear friend and partner, Kingsly, his wife, Anita, his dear parents, Babu, and all the dear pastors and workers who do the most important work of leading people to Jesus!

But above all, I would like to thank my wife, Antje, who has always stood by me while I was away so often. Without her, this would not have been possible.

And last, but not least: our Lord Jesus Christ, who has taken my heart captive to do this beautiful work with Kingsly. All honor to Him above all and to Him who has worked in us.

INTRODUCTION

I t was a great joy to write this book. I had to dig into the treasure chest of my golden memories to remember all the amazing things God has done in and through the work of Abba Child Care over the past twenty years.

It all started because God called two totally different men that He brought together for a purpose beyond their wildest dreams. Neither of us had any idea what it would become, neither can we take credit for all the great things God has done through our union.

This book tells the amazing story of Abba Child Care, founded by Kingsly Lazarus from South India and Jaap Dieleman from the Netherlands, who God used to create a winning team for the glory of God and for the blessing of millions in India.

Kingsly Lazarus, born into a poor Christian family in South India as the first-born son, was declared dead in his mother's womb after a tragic accident but was resurrected from the dead because of his mother's promise to care for widows, orphans, and the poor. Because of her promise, his destiny in life was already determined. He married Anita, born to a poor Dalit family, but against all odds, was adopted as a child by a wealthy, high-caste Hindu family. There, she grew up to be a brilliant gospel singer.

I was born into a middle-class business family in the Netherlands and lost my father when I was thirteen years old. The loss of my father caused me to lose my way and become addicted to drugs until I almost died. But then God called me out of darkness into His marvelous light to be a father to the fatherless and an evangelist to the nations. I have written over thirty books, traveled the world, and preached Christ to millions of people. I married Antje, my wife of Indonesian descent but born in the Netherlands. She is a great cook, specializing in Moluccan cuisine.

The most unlikely combination, Kingsly and I, were miraculously linked together to accomplish the plan God had for us. As the Bible says, one shall slay a thousand, and two shall slay ten thousand (Deuteronomy 32:30). We have seen God's mighty hand in miracle after miracle. The things that God has done are beyond our imagination and wildest expectations.

Only the highlights have been recorded in this book. To tell of everything that happened in those many years and the many lives involved would become a library of many books. I hope you will be inspired and convinced that He can do through you what God did through two simple boys as you read these amazing stories.

Enjoy our exciting story and be blessed.

CHAPTER 1

THE DAY OF SMALL BEGINNINGS

E very story must begin somewhere.

Ours began a few decades ago in the heartland of Tamilnadu, South India. There lived a man named Koman. We know little about him, but we know he was a medicine man. He grew up in an animistic Hindu community. He didn't know any better. But one day, he heard the message of the gospel, and it spoke to his hungry, seeking soul, and Koman made the decision to give his life to Christ. Then, he changed his name to Thomas.

After Thomas gave his life to Jesus Christ, he began to serve Him to the best of his ability. Little did he know that his decision would set in motion a miracle story that would continue to this day through his son, his grandson, his great-grandson, and many more.

Thomas married his sweetheart, and in due time, she became pregnant and gave birth to a boy. They named him John. Deeply convinced of God's love for life, he joyfully raised John in his new found faith in Jesus Christ. Through his upbringing in the faith and love of Jesus, little John developed a love for God and the work of the Lord. It was no surprise that later in life, he became a pastor and planted a church in the southern region of Chennai called The Healing Gospel Church. Later, the church's remarkable role in the development of this story becomes apparent. John was very devoted to Christ, and with the help of Christ for the Nations, he founded his first church south of Chennai. His zeal for God eventually led him to establish six more churches. In time, John married his beloved Lydia, and they had a son whom they named Lazarus.

Because of God's love that burned in their hearts and their compassion for children, they adopted an orphan boy into their home and named him Silas. Silas grew up as a brother to Lazarus since they were about the same age. In fact, little Lazarus only knew Silas as his little brother.

Growing up in the church, Lazarus loved the things of God, especially singing. At first, he sang the psalms and hymns he heard in church, but there were songs in his own heart that he began to compose and sing as he preached the gospel. In time, Lazarus became a very effective evangelist, operating in the gifts of prophecy and deliverance, preaching the word of God, and singing his songs wherever he went. It was no surprise that he began to produce his own music, and his songs are now sung in churches all over India, even as far as Sri Lanka. To date, he has produced over eighteen albums. As a young man, he fell in love with the beautiful Rachel, and they got married. They were poor but served the Lord with all their hearts and all their talents as they traveled through the land teaching, preaching, and singing to the glory of God.

As a young couple, they wanted to start a family of their own, and after a while, Rachel became pregnant, and they eagerly awaited the birth of their first child. But around the sixth month of her pregnancy, they were hit by a large bus while riding their motorcycle. Rachel fell off the motorcycle and onto the road. She was rushed to a nearby hospital, where doctors examined her. "Madam, I have good news and bad news for you!" the doctor said. "The good news is that you have not broken any bones or suffered any serious injuries—just a few scratches that will heal quickly." The doctor continued, "The bad news, however, is that I cannot hear your baby's heartbeat. Because you fell on your stomach, I fear that the child is either dead or has serious brain damage. If it is born alive, it will be a 'vegetable', a zombie. Therefore, I advise you to terminate this pregnancy for your own health and safety."

Rachel received the message as a nightmare, shocked and stunned by this heartbreaking news. For a few seconds, she didn't know what to do. "Please give us some time to think about what we should do, doctor!" They went home, heartbroken by the tragic accident that had happened that day. At home, they got down on their knees and began to cry out to God. He had given them this pregnancy, not to give birth to a brain-dead baby, or worse . . . a dead baby. "Please, God, let my child live. I did not get pregnant to give birth to a dead baby." In her desperation, she made a promise to God. "Please, God, let my child live, and I promise you that when our child is born healthy, we will take care of orphans and widows!"

Despite the advice of the doctors, Lazarus and Rachel decided not to abort the baby but to trust God.

And so this amazing story began.

RAISED IN THE WOMB

Their faith and trust in God did not go unnoticed, nor did their prayers go unanswered, because a little while later, Rachel gave birth to a perfectly healthy boy, whom they named Kingsly. Imagine this: He was declared dead in the womb by the doctors but was brought back to life by God in the womb. On top of that, Kingsly's last name is Lazarus. Lazarus of the Bible was raised from the grave, but Kingsly Lazarus was raised in his mother's womb. Wow! Who could have thought of something like that? This is a typical trademark of our God.

Rachel did not experience a single consequence because of the promise she made to God.

As the story unfolds, you will see that her promise has changed the course of history, not only for herself but for hundreds, even thousands of people—and to this day! Who knows how far that influence will extend into the future!

A few months after Kingsly's birth in 1979, Rachel remembered the promise she had made to God. So, Lazarus and Rachel began to take in some children.

One of the first children was Babu. His mother was a widow and could not take care of him. Therefore, she took Babu with joy to Lazarus' and Rachel's home. Little Kingsly, about two years old, suddenly had an older brother. They grew up together as real brothers, just as Lazarus' father had grown up with Silas.

Like Silas, Babu plays a remarkable role in this story. After Babu, many more orphans followed, as Rachel had promised God. But of all the children, Babu has remained the closest to the family to this day and is even an integral part of the ministry to serve the widows and orphans—all stemming from Rachel's promise to God.

When Babu came of age, he married Selvi. They had a daughter, Priyanka. As an orphan himself who grew up in a loving home full of compassion for orphans, Babu was struck by the same love for orphans. So, it comes as no surprise that, eventually, he and Selvi adopted an orphan boy into their family. They named him Andrew.

As you can see, ever since Kingsly's grandfather adopted Silas, the passion and love for orphans and widows have run in the blood of their family. Silas later became the caretaker (father) for the orphans in the orphanage that Lazarus and Rachel started. Kingsly's father adopted Babu, who is now Kingsly's right hand in his great ministry to the poor, widows, and orphans. Babu then went on to adopt another orphan. And so it goes. That is God's great heartbeat, for He is the Father of all life and a Father to the fatherless. How wonderful it has been to see God's heartbeat become visible in this amazing story.

Born into a poor family and later adopted into a high-caste Hindu household, Kingsly's wife, Anita, has a remarkable Cinderella-like story. Kingsly and Anita would continue the family legacy and follow in the footsteps of his ancestors to love and care for the poor, the needy, the orphans, and the widows.

However, to prepare him for that work, his story starts at a Bible school in England.

Kingsly had no idea what God had in store for him, as this was the day of only small beginnings, as we shall see in the next chapter.

CHAPTER 2

THE DUTCH CONNECTION

As a little boy, Kingsly played with his toys under the dining table while his father sat and talked with well-known preachers such as T. L. Osborn, John Osteen, Dr. Dinakaran, Johan Maasbach, Lester Sumrall, and others. As just a little boy, he sat playing at the feet of these men of God but had no idea of the mighty plans God had in store for him. However, he would end up following in the footsteps of these men of God to step into those plans.

When Kingsly grew up and began to follow in his father's footsteps, his father felt that he needed an education. Because of their connection to the Maasbach family, they sent Kingsly to Robert Maasbach's Bible School in Kent, England, in 1999. It was difficult for this young man to survive in the cold and foggy climate of England with little support. To support himself, he found a job in a fast-food restaurant and often lived on leftovers to save money. Although he did miss his favorite spicy Indian dishes such as chapatis, dahl, and biryani, he managed to survive and complete Bible School.

On the day the students proudly and gratefully received their diplomas, a fellow Dutch student, Maaike de Keizer from Vlissingen, invited Kingsly to come and stay for a few days in Vlissingen. He agreed and spent a few days with the De Keizer family and spoke at their church. The Dutch food was horrible to his Indian tongue, so he pretended to fast so that he wouldn't have to admit his distaste for the tasteless Dutch food. However, to satisfy his hunger, he pretended to go for a walk, and hoping no one would see him sneak into a Chinese restaurant to enjoy some spicy Asian food.

Oh, how delicious it was to eat spicy chicken! "Forgive me, O God!" he said to the Lord.

During his stay with the Keizer family, he visited the Maasbach World Mission Centre in The Hague and the Euro-Spirit conference in Amsterdam. He enjoyed his stay with the De Keizer family, who were so kind and caring. Father De Keizer also introduced Kingsly to the Christian Centre Zeeland, another church in Vlissingen, who invited him to preach at a Sunday service.

After the service, Kingsly met a small Indonesian woman who responded to his sermon with great joy. She ran to him and enthusiastically told him about her husband, who was also a preacher and missionary who worked regularly in India. She wanted Kingsly to meet her husband.

Father de Keizer knew me personally and agreed that Kingsly and I should meet. Kingsly was curious because he knew I was on a mission. He had seen my photo and heard all sorts of remarkable stories; however, I had remained a mystery to him. God's timing to meet each other had not yet arrived. Only God knew what would come out of our meeting.

WHO IS THIS MYSTERIOUS MAN?

Kingsly took the train from Schiphol Airport to Vlissingen the next time Kingsly visited the Netherlands. To his surprise, I had just entered the train station while he was leaving the station. I was with my wife, whom he recognized from the church in Vlissingen. Kingsly was so excited to finally meet me, but apologetically, I said, "I have to catch my train; otherwise, I will miss my flight because I am leaving for a mission trip to Kenya. Hopefully, we will meet again next time!" And I left.

Everything Kingsly heard about me made him more and more curious, yet we still couldn't come to know each other even after having met in person! Kingsly was disappointed. It wasn't until his next visit to the Netherlands, in 2006, when Kingsly's host would coordinate a meeting between him and me. I was rather reluctant to meet with Kingsly because I had several bad experiences with Indian preachers, so I proceeded with caution. However, after our meeting, I gave Kingsly some of my sermons and said: "Please listen to these messages and let me know if I can bless you with the things that God has entrusted to me!" I expected nothing from this conversation, but God was preparing my heart for something much greater than I could have ever imagined.

Contrary to my expectations, I later received a message from Kingsly that I would be a great blessing if I would come and equip the church leaders of India to minister "the Father heart of God." So, the plan was made to speak at five major leadership conferences in the major cities of Chennai, Bombay, Calcutta, New Delhi, and Bangalore. I was very excited because I felt called to it. Neither of us expected God to use this appointment for a much greater purpose, which would unfold in the years to come.

And so, I decided to travel to India.

Although I was primarily focused on evangelism and equipping leaders, the Lord had more recently spoken to me about His love for orphans, widows, and the poor. Some time prior to my trip, my eyes were opened to these target groups. I realized that serving these groups is a vital aspect of the good news and had been insufficiently addressed in my ministry. Convinced by Matthew 25:40 (author paraphrase): "Truly I say to you, insofar as you did it to one of the least of these brothers of mine, you did it to me," I became the hands and feet of this assignment. However, I did not realize that my commitment to the very poorest in Kosovo was only preparation for a much greater work that God would entrust to me in India. The more I invested in my assignment, the more I was filled with love and passion for the very poorest, and I wanted to commit to serving this target group. It was as if God had to wait for my heart to catch up before he would open the door to India.

In preparation for my trip to India, God spoke to me prophetically, lifting a tip of the veil. On separate occasions, two friends told me that I would do many aid projects in India. I laughed because I was convinced my only assignment there was to speak to leaders. I had not yet realized that God had another plan that would become apparent very quickly in the first part of my journey.

Kingsly and I have been working together as partners ever since. Today, our ministry has grown beyond anything we could have expected, and it continues to grow to this day. As the story progresses, new visions appear on the horizon, and I invite you to step on board and travel with us through time to see God's never-ending goodness, guidance, and grace. May God inspire you to write your own story with Him as you read ours.

But I'm getting ahead of myself. Let's go back to the moment Kingsly invited me to join him in India, where our first journey together began.

CHAPTER 3
THE JOURNEY BEGINS

Every journey begins with a first step.

Though Kingsly had only asked me to help with leadership conferences in India, God gave me a glimpse into His plans for me the Saturday night before my departure when my friend revealed God's intention to use me in more aid projects. Kosovo was only the beginning. The following Sunday morning, another dear friend of mine spoke tearfully about two passion projects God would have me undertake in India. Two different men who did not even know each other prophesied exactly the same thing. Just like the Bible, God confirms His plans for people more than once to get our attention!

With those prophetic words still ringing in my ears, I boarded the plane to India. God would later confirm these prophetic words, contrary to my agenda. What was in store for me? What new adventures would I experience with God? Was God's agenda completely different than mine? I was unsure, but I stored my friends' messages in my heart anyway. "When I arrive, I will follow God's lead," I said to myself. One thing was certain: I knew that I was on the right track. I had been caught in the web of God's love, and He would certainly show me what He wanted—I only had to follow the flow of His love.

On November 6, 2008, I arrived around midnight in Chennai, a city of millions in southeast India on the Bay of Bengal, formerly known as Madras. My team members Wichard and Ulfert had traveled ahead of me, and Kingsly had a whole program lined up for them. We would speak at various leadership conferences in different cities and travel more than 5,000 kilometers throughout India to equip leaders, visit churches, and encourage believers.

Blessed Generations

I stayed with Kingsly and his parents and received an exceptionally warm welcome. It didn't take long before I felt completely at home. I noticed that many people lived on their property; they had an orphanage, and they cared for the poor, elderly, single mothers, and widows. Kingsley's father told me that Kingsly was the fourth generation in his family to serve Christ. John, Kingsly's father, was given a broad mission to travel all over India, hold large campaigns, and plant many churches. It quickly became clear to me that Kingsly was a special man with a very important calling on his life. I knew that Kingsly carried a remarkable anointing and that God blessed his work greatly.

Kingsly has a Bible school and provides regional training days and leaders' conferences across India. What an impressive ministry for a young man who was barely thirty at the time! He could have been my son. The more I spent time with Kingsly, the more impressed I became with his work, but I didn't learn Kingsly's secret until two days later.

A TRAGIC ACCIDENT AND A PROMISE TO GOD

I spoke in Kingsly's church on that first Sunday in India. My message was about caring for orphans and widows because it had been so heavy on my heart. Kingsly was speaking at another church that day, but his mother was present. Through heavy sobs, I saw how deeply the message had touched her. After the message, she thanked me and took me aside. "I have to tell you why we started caring for orphans and widows." I began to listen attentively to her story.

"John and I got married and were busy with our work for the Lord. It wasn't long before I became pregnant for the first time."

"We were looking forward to parenthood and greatly anticipated the arrival of our first child. John was busy speaking at various evangelistic campaigns and conferences. I was riding on the back of his moped on the way to a meeting one day when the accident happened—we were hit by a bus. The moped was completely crushed, but fortunately, we escaped unscathed. Nevertheless, we wanted be on the safe side, so we went to the hospital for a check-up."

"After the doctor examined me, he said: 'Madam, I have good news and bad news! The good news is that you have not broken anything or suffered any serious injuries, but the bad news is that your baby did not survive the impact. I advise you to have the baby removed as soon as possible for the sake of your own health.' I was completely paralyzed when I heard the bad news. It was as if my stomach turned and my heart broke. Shocked and in tears, I asked the doctor for a day to process the bad news. In our anguish, we cried out to God for the life of our child."

> # WHEN OUR CHILD LIVES, WE WILL TAKE CARE OF THE POOR, THE WIDOWS, AND THE ORPHANS.

Rachel shared the promise to God and said, "Dear God, I cannot believe that I have to give birth to a dead child. I ask you that our child may live and I promise you that when our child lives, we will take care of the poor, the widows and the orphans. Amen!"

Then her heart was at peace and she was able to surrender it to God.

Raised from the Dead

"The next day we went back to the hospital. The doctor examined me again and looked a little confused. He put the stethoscope on my belly again and listened attentively. Finally he said completely astonished: "Unbelievable I hear a …, heartbeat again! Yet I know for sure that yesterday there was no heartbeat, but now there is! It is a miracle, but your child is alive!" The adrenaline was pumping through my veins, I was tense with happy excitement and could not wait to tell John the good news, that God had performed a miracle and that our baby was alive. We could not contain our joy, it was something so unimaginable, so special, so unspeakable. Our God had raised our baby from the dead in my mother's womb. Not long after that our first child was born, a healthy son ... our Kingsly.

> ## LAZARUS FROM THE BIBLE WAS RAISED IN THE GRAVE, KINGSLY LAZARUS WAS RAISED IN THE WOMB.

Rachel beamed as she told me the story, and I cried. What a story, and what a miracle—Kingsly had been raised from the dead in the womb! Wow!

And then his name: Kingsly Lazarus. How can you think of something like that? Just as Lazarus was raised from the dead while he was in the grave, Kingsly was also raised from the dead while he was still in his mother's womb. Wow! And that happened in answer to Rachel's prayer and the promise to care for orphans and widows. When you make a promise like that to God, you touch a very sensitive chord in His heart. A promise like that is irresistible to Him. I felt the special presence of God on and around Kingsly.

Caring for Orphans and Widows

John and Rachel had made a promise to God, and not a small one either. In a poor country like India, orphans and widows have nothing at all because they are not accepted by their environment. But they kept their word and started their orphanage, the "Sharing Hands Foundation," managing it alongside all of their other ministry work.

A visit to one of their orphanages was inevitable after the conversation with Kingsly's mother. I wondered if this was perhaps what God had meant when He spoke about the two projects in India. I did not yet realize that it was Kingsly himself—and not just his apostolic work in India—that would solidify my love and fuel my lifelong mission to care for orphans and widows.

Rachel then shared: "I remembered our promise to God and wondered how we could follow through on our word. That's when we opened the door of our little house and the door of our hearts to receive orphans." Babu came along, then a second, and a third, and so on. "At that moment, we began to feed about a thousand mouths every day—orphans and widows, the poor and beggars on the streets, and lepers and other needy people."

I was deeply moved when I heard Rachel's story. Tears streamed down my cheeks, and a lump formed in my throat. I was indeed lured into "God's trap" as His passion for the poorest of the poor gripped my heart.

While Rachel shared her story, God spoke very clearly to me:

"I didn't just raise this child from the dead for the mother but also, for the countless number of orphans and widows who would receive love and care through her because of the promise she made to Me!"

More tears rolled down my cheeks, and my heart began to break. The child Rachel carried in her womb, Kingsly, would be the fulfillment of her promise to God.

I was received with great honor during my first visit to their Chennai orphanage. The children sang songs and performed small plays. I was touched to hear them pray and share the heart-breaking stories of their tragic background, but the children received love, care, food, and education there. They beamed and were so grateful because the orphanage gave these beautiful little ones a future. I had a child hanging on every finger, and I could have "eaten" them up. The children were so endearing, so hopeful, and so thankful. God's love was palpable in that beautiful place.

I wondered how the orphanage fit into God's promise to me.

BAPATLA

Our plan was to travel through India for leadership meetings in different cities on my first weekend there, but my back began to hurt so severely that traveling on India's rough roads became unbearable. After a few days and almost a thousand kilometers of driving, we arrived at the town of Bapatla, where Sharing Hands had also started a small orphanage. We would spend the night there to recharge a bit and then visit the orphanage the next day.

The orphanage started with ten orphans. But after the tsunami, which also hit the coast of Bapatla, twenty orphans were left behind without parents at the police station. They asked Sharing Hands if they would take them in. Kingsly couldn't say no, so suddenly, he had thirty children to care for! Since then, the work has grown, and now, the orphanage cares for over fifty children.

The only downside was that the living conditions were down-right miserable. The boys slept on a dirt floor in a small, shabby church hall, and the girls slept in a nearby house. There was no electricity or running water, only a hand pump. There were no beds or lockers. In fact, there was little to nothing except the love that Kingsly and his family gave them. It was clear they needed help.

"Can't you get anything better than this?" I asked Kingsly. "We do what we can with what we have, but we've never turned a child away!" Kingsly said. He told me that they had a nice piece of land in mind to build a better home but no money to buy it. Moved by their need, I invited Kingsly to join me in a search for good land. We soon found a piece of land for sale that was even nicer than the one Kingsly had set his sights on. I told Kingsly, "You know what? We are going to buy that land and build a beautiful house for these precious little children!" I consulted with my Dutch teammates to explore sources of assistance.

Then, it suddenly dawned on me that this was one of the projects God had referred to!

I wanted to know a little more about the children, so I had Kingsly share their backgrounds with me.

Six-year-old Angel and four-year-old Sofia were abandoned by their parents. Lanvanya, a beautiful six-year-old girl, was found begging for food on the streets because both her parents were dying of AIDS. Prabhakar's mother had tried to commit suicide three times after his father ran off with another woman.

Blessy's father and mother died in a car accident. Sisters T. Blessy and Marry-Stella were abandoned by their mentally ill mother and drunken father. Saravanthi's and Ananda Babu's father was brutally murdered in front of their mother, and the confusion and heartbreak made caring for them an impossibility. Not to mention many others, each with their own story.

Some lost their parents in the tsunami; others were found in a box on Kingsly's doorstep in the morning, and others were "secretly" left at his church.

But now they had all fortunately been given a future in this home, where they were lovingly cared for and learned about the love of the Heavenly Father. Although the children were well cared for there, their humble shelter stood in stark contrast to their radiant smiles. As I looked at these children, God knocked me out with a special revelation of His love. It was as if I had heard His voice deep inside me ask:

Do you want to take care of them? Will you take care of them?

I could have said no, I didn't want to. I had to think of the moment when Jesus was hanging on the cross and said to Mary, "Woman, behold your son!" and to John, "Son, behold your mother!"

Imagine Jesus dying in excruciating pain on the cross, carrying all the sins of this world on His neck. But in the midst of all His suffering, He still thought of the welfare of His mother, Mary, who was a widow. It seems Jesus was thinking about who would care for His mother when He was no longer there. Then he saw John, the only disciple of His who stood by His side at the cross. He had lain on His breast and heard the heartbeat of Jesus, and in that moment, I was hearing His heartbeat, too. Jesus loved John very much and knew that He could trust him, so He entrusted His mother's care to him.

The Bible says that at that hour, John took her into his home and cared for her. He could not go to social services. There was no widow's pension. No, John cared for her as a son cares for his mother. How much confidence must Jesus have had in John to entrust His mother's care to him?

When I thought about this story, I was deeply impressed by the love of Jesus, and now, it was as if Jesus was impressing the same thing on me when I saw the children of Bapatla.

I could entrust John to care for Mary. And now I ask you, My son, do you see these children? Can I entrust you to care for them?

My heart broke. Jesus's voice was irresistible. I could not say no and did not want to. "Yes, Lord!" I said, with tears in my eyes. "With your help, I will take care of these children!" I made my decision. I didn't know all that Jesus had in store, but I was determined to do whatever Jesus asked me to do.

CALCULATE THE COSTS

No sooner had I said "yes" to the Lord than I felt sick and threw up. I suddenly had a splitting headache and terrible back pain. When I returned to my lodging, I collapsed and didn't know where I was.

I became sicker by the hour, so sick that the rest of the team feared for my life. I dreaded the thought of traveling thousands of miles over the bad roads of India in this poor condition. Kingsly consulted with his father, who thought it advisable to cancel the leaders' conferences and fly me back to Chennai. He didn't want to think about sending me back to the Netherlands in a coffin. It seemed as if the devil was trying to nip God's plan in the bud.

Kingsly's father feared that this would be the first and last time I would come to India. However, his fear was unrealized because I had heard the voice of God and was determined to follow it, whatever the cost. I was forced to fly back to Chennai, while the rest of the team followed by car.

I found the situation very annoying and felt like a loser. In retrospect, I do see the hand of God in it. Ulfert, one of my team members, was a project leader and had a lot of building knowledge. Now that I had to rest anyway, his expertise came in handy as he effortlessly planned for the construction, giving us time to brainstorm together about the children's home we wanted to build.

Kingsley and I started doing just that. We made sketches, shared ideas, and discussed what it should look like. How big should the rooms be? How many children would sleep in each room? How big should the dining room and playground be? How many toilets and showers did we need? And how many children could we help? Initially, the home was intended to house one hundred children, but if we made the foundations strong enough, we could always build a few more floors on top later.

We calculated the size of the rooms and how many children could fit in each one. We sketched how they should look and how much land we would need. Our heads were buzzing, but our creative efforts were rewarded because gradually, our dream began to take shape. In our minds, this children's home was already a reality.

CHAPTER 4

ABBA CHILDREN'S HOME

We didn't want to call our children's home an orphanage, that would only label the residents as nothing but orphans. But they are so much more than that. After all, God is their Father, and we embody the love of the Heavenly Father. That Father is called Abba in the Bible. No, not the pop group Abba from Sweden, but the Hebrew word *Abba*, which actually means "Daddy." So, we decided to call it the Abba Children's House because God wants to be a Father to the fatherless.

But as the picture became clearer, the cost of building and preparing the home also became clearer, and the costs were high. Together with the purchase of the land and the construction of the house, including the finishing, we came to more than €100,000—much more than we had initially thought. On top of that, it was my first time doing such a large project.

But if you say A, you must also say B, and so there was no way back. I would ask myself, "Where do I get that much money from?" Yet my heart was at ease. I knew for sure that the Lord wanted us to take care of these children, and this was the first step. So, to put my money where my mouth was, I transferred the first €5,000 to Sharing Hands that same evening because then I could not go back if, for whatever reason, I was tempted to change my mind.

We also felt the €100,000 budget for one hundred children was quite nice because then it would only cost €1,000 per child.

Now that we had come this far, the natural question was how we would care for the children. We only had to build a house once, but those mouths had to be fed every day. So, we started to brainstorm and calculate again. How much does it cost to feed a child and provide clothing, education, medical care, and something a little extra? Kingsly knew several children were already in their care. We thought €15 per child per month was very meager. So, after consultation, we decided to increase this amount to €25 per month per child. For this amount, a child would get a loving home but also food, clothing, education, and medical care. All inclusive!

But more questions remained: who would maintain contact with the sponsors and connect with the sponsored children? Who would collect the money and send it to India? Who would run the administrative side? I knew not to do it myself even though I wanted to help. Fortunately, Ulfert saw a challenge in this, so with his organization, Multimissions, he would sponsor the children. Without realizing it, right away, we had also launched our second project. Exactly as the Lord had said.

But this was only the beginning. The Lord had spoken that I would do many things and that these two projects would confirm that I was on the right track. By the time our time in India was over, I was well enough to travel, and the plans for the building were all set.

> ## IT WAS TIME TO GET MOVING— THERE WAS WORK TO BE DONE.

The Lord had "set me up" again, but I didn't mind at all. I consider it all a great adventure to make others happy, and in doing so make Jesus happy, because what you do for one of the least of His, you do for Him!

Despite all the emotional commotion, it was time to get moving—there was work to be done. The land had been purchased, the construction drawing was ready, and the building permit had been issued. Construction started in early April 2009. There were already about twenty-five interested parties who wanted to sponsor a child. The project was fueled by more than just emotion and "movement;" we had to roll up our sleeves to make that beautiful dream come true. We still had a long way to go.

These moments are quite the adventures that start with a passion in our heart, a thought, or a dream, a dream that God Himself will bring to fruition because He has said that He will do things that no eye has seen and that have not entered the heart of man (see 1 Corinthians 2:9). He wants to exceed our wildest expectations and give us more than we can ask or think, if only we have the courage to dream. So, dare to see the invisible, and you will discover that God will do the impossible.

When the vision became clear and we had calculated the costs, I came to the shocking conclusion that the entire project would cost even more than €100,000. I had never done such a big project before and was a little afraid I would be unable to accomplish this dream. It felt like an impossible challenge, as if I had to walk on water. Just like Peter, I had to keep my eyes on Jesus to do the impossible to "just" walk on water.

ABBA CHILDREN HOME

It took a while to get all the money we needed because the whole thing, together with the playground and the school bus, would cost €120,000. This was a huge challenge, bigger than I had ever had before. However, I accepted the challenge and started raising money when I returned to the Netherlands. Initially, I used my evangelical organization, De Heilbode, to raise funds for this project but felt these new projects might be a conflict of interest with our original ministry. Therefore, I considered setting up a new foundation to carry them out.

I returned to India the following year to monitor the construction progress, a period during which my confidence in securing the money on time was tested. Slowly but surely, this dream became a reality—the next time I visited India, the Abba Children Home had officially opened.

This trip was unusually joyful because three of my children accompanied me. They were so inspired that they composed several original songs for the project.

My daughter-in-law, Jonne, wrote the lyrics and my son, Jozua, wrote the music. Together, with a few very good Indian musicians that Kingsly recruited, they recorded three beautiful songs in the studio in no time, a unique mix of western jazz with the Indian sitar and tabla. The opening of the Abba Children Home was a big party because the dream had now become reality. However, there was little time to daydream about this success.

In the meantime, Kingsly also had a project running with orphans in Orissa. The parents of these children were brutally slaughtered during the great massacre in 2008. At the same time, he helped save orphans from the granite mines in Rajasthan. In his enthusiasm, Kingsly asked me to join him in these projects. Although I wanted to, I hesitated because I had not yet completed the project in Guntur. But from the moment Kingsly asked me to participate, I had already said "yes" in my heart.

It would not be long before I would travel to both places.

God was saying, "I want you to think bigger!"

Back in the Netherlands, I began to investigate the global problem of orphans, child trafficking, child prostitution, child sacrifice, slavery, and infanticide of female babies, especially in India and China. I was so overwhelmed and shocked by what I found.

According to my findings, there are approximately 150 million orphans and half-orphans. Even more shocking is that one-third of these 150 million children live in the streets and slums of India. Although our efforts to help had saved over a hundred children, this number seemed insignificant in light of the overwhelming number of orphans in India. My achievement seemed so insignificant, like a drop in the ocean.

Although we had reached one hundred orphan children, I was more concerned about those I had NOT reached than the ones I had reached. I felt like the shepherd who left the ninety-nine sheep to go and find the lost one. I heard the silent whisper of God's heartbeat for those still outside.

What could I do for them? How could I reach them? How could I answer the cry of these children? I had done good things, but I wanted to do more. My vision and reach were certainly being expanded, so my faith and finances had to be stretched as well.

So, the next time I went to India, Kingsly and I visited the projects in Orissa and Rajasthan. The number of children in Orissa had risen to over 300, and the number of children in Rajasthan was growing even faster—to several hundred from an initial fifty. We needed a good facility to accommodate all the orphans. So, we started dreaming about buying land and building a place for them. Inspired by God's words—"think bigger"—Kingsly and I dreamt about building a village. And so the vision of "Abba Village" was born.

CHAPTER 5

ABBA VILLAGE RAJASTHAN

G od was constantly stretching my faith to think bigger. Because I was known as an evangelist, it was already a big change and challenge to convince my team and sponsors that God's Spirit was leading me to accept this transition in my ministry.

In addition, the need arose for a new organization. Until now, I had operated under the banner of my evangelistic ministry called "Herald of the Good News," but I needed something different for the social and developmental needs of the children based on biblical norms and values. Finding support for those specific needs under the new organization would be easier and would evade the conflict of interest with my evangelistic ministry. Therefore, I created a new foundation in 2013 called "Abba Child Care International."

When I registered Abba Child Care International, God spoke a very specific word to me as I prepared to return to India. I already knew that God had been telling me to think bigger and feed the hungry, just as He had spoken to the disciples to test their faith. He wanted them to be aware of the need for food and work to meet that need. So, Jesus told His disciples to feed the people. When they did the math, they found that they did not have enough money to feed everyone—not even a small bite. In the same way, I found the challenge enormous and the need far too great to handle.

However, Jesus only did this to test them. After all, He knew what He was going to do. He wanted to involve them and show up as their Provider. Immediately, He multiplied the little boy's five loaves and two fish to feed a great multitude.

Many times, I felt just like the disciples, realizing that it was, in fact, an impossible task on my own. Yet, I also felt like the little boy who gave everything into the hands of Jesus, and with the gift of that little boy, Jesus performed the miracle of multiplication to feed them all.

Right as I was about to leave for India, the Lord spoke to me: "My son, this whole project of loving and caring for the widows and orphans is not your project. It is My project! I have tested and challenged you to see its necessity. But you cannot carry this burden, and I do not ask you to do so. The only thing I ask of you is to be My partner!"

I burst into tears and was deeply moved when I realized that I had tried to carry an unbearable weight on my shoulders. When the Lord told me that it was His vision, His dream, and His passion to do this, I felt so honored that He had included me to participate with Him in His beautiful work. It was as if the burden of the world had been lifted from my shoulders, but the vision and mission remained. Now it would be different because I realized that it was God's passion to love and care for the poor, the needy, the widows, and the orphans of India, of which there are so many.

So, I was challenged to trust God for the impossible. For that reason, 'Abba Child Care' was now officially registered, to handle all financial matters and other interests through this channel. I left for India with renewed vision, new energy, and new strength to strive for better and bigger things. Yes, I would put my hand to the plow, but my Heavenly Father would pay the bill for what it cost to fulfill His dreams. So, let us think big and go for the best. With this renewed vision, I left for India again and visited Rajasthan with Kingsly. God wanted to do big things, so we said, "Let us build a village and call it 'Abba Village.'"

ABBA VILLAGE

Kingsly was immediately drawn to the vision, so we started to make plans to build a village with forty houses. Each house would accommodate twenty-five children and a couple to care for them. There would also be a sports field, a common hall, a dining hall, a medical unit, a school, and gardens. In the meantime, we found an architect who wanted to design it for free. He drew the blueprint for the entire village, including all the facilities. I still have these drawings. I approached organizations and NGOs that often sponsor and invest money in non-profits, such as Wilde Ganzen and the Postcode Lottery. We bought the first piece of land, started building the walls, drilled for water, and installed electricity on the plot.

But suddenly, the tide turned, and the wind changed.

Wilde Ganzen withdrew. The Postcode Lottery demanded that we not talk about Jesus and asked us to advertise for them. We didn't feel right about doing that and wanted to give all the glory to the Lord, so we withdrew from these sponsors. In addition, the owner of the second piece of land decided to raise the price exorbitantly because he distrusted us and thought we were rich, Western investors who would now buy the land only to sell it later for a lot of money. No matter what we said, we could not convince them of our pure and selfless motives. Moreover, several local Christian groups discouraged us from building this village because they expected that the majority of the Hindu community would object to it, since they consider orphans to be a curse. It seemed that the whole project went from excitement to disappointment in a matter of days. What were we to do now?

We trusted God for His provision no matter what! Peter had spent the whole night fishing and caught nothing. The Lord told him to throw his net on the other side of the boat. So, that's what we did, too. We threw the net to the other side of the boat.

> THE WHOLE PROJECT WENT FROM EXCITEMENT TO DISAPPOINTMENT IN A MATTER OF DAYS.

Throwing the net to the other side of the boat

At first, we thought this was the work of the devil to hinder and oppose God's plan. Maybe that was the case. But how much more, then, will our God work ALL THINGS together for good to those who love Him and are called according to His purpose? Doesn't "all things" include adversities?

At that time, we had no idea that something good could come from something so bad. Was that really possible? Yes, it was. We soon found out that God knew what was best for us much more than we did.

Peter's vision for catching fish was good, but God taught Peter a new strategy that he had never done before. As a third-generation fisherman, he knew that you should fish at night, not during the day. It was unheard of to cast the net at the wrong time and on the wrong side of the boat. But because Jesus told him to do it, Peter did what he normally would not do, like an eagle throwing its young out of the nest to teach it to fly. Just like Peter, our vision was good, but God had a better strategy, so He threw us out of our comfort zone and into a new adventure.

Dowry in India

We became aware of the female infanticide happening, a terribly dark secret in Indian culture, caused by the Hindu tradition of dowry.

A dowry is a payment, such as a piece of land or money, given by the groom's family to the bride's family at the time of marriage. This is how it works in most African countries and is the most important tradition. However, it is the exact opposite in India. In India, the bride's family has to give a huge dowry to the *groom's* family, not the other way around. Because of this outdated tradition, most families do not want daughters for fear that they will cost them a fortune and rob them of their wealth if they get married. At that point, they lose both their daughter and their wealth. However, this tradition is still widely practiced by most Hindus of every caste. For this reason, many see a baby girl as a curse. To avoid this curse, they abort the girl before birth. However, the central government has banned abortion to prevent this genocide. Nevertheless, rich people will try to bribe doctors to scan for gender and abort the baby if she is a girl.

Poor people can't afford this expensive procedure, so they kill the child, throw it away, bury it alive, or let the dog eat it to destroy the evidence of the horrific crime.

Fathers who discover their wives are pregnant with a girl often pressure the mother to abort or somehow dispose of the child to avoid "the curse." Some men even kill both their wives and daughters.

Most women would rather leave their baby girl in the hospital, hoping that someone will care for her, than risk taking the baby home only to have the father kill her.

It sounds unbelievable to people in the Western world, but we have infallible evidence of these horrific crimes. In the case of infanticide, we see one baby boy dying against 122 baby girls in India. It is abundantly clear that this horrific practice is behind such a large discrepancy. Shocked and horrified by these facts, Kingsly and I decided that before Christmas of that year, we would rescue at least ten baby girls and place them in foster homes who would embrace, adopt, and love them as their own.

At the same time, God used a friend from the Netherlands to donate €10,000 with the explicit purpose of buying land for ten poor Dalit families, who would then adopt one of our rescued baby girls. So, each family had a piece of land worth €1,000 to grow crops to generate a basic income. We killed two birds with one stone with this plan because that donation would help ten poor Dalit families and ten helpless baby girls at once. It was a win-win situation for two needy parties.

Kingsly and Anita had two sons, but they also wanted a daughter. Their wish, however, did not come true until they were moved by God's love to care for these little girls whose own mothers couldn't care for them. Yes, God opened Anita's womb to receive a baby girl of her own. They named her Anna. We all saw this as God's confirmation and approval of our response to His heart for these innocent little baby girls.

> ## THROUGH THAT SPECIAL DONATION, GOD SHOWED US A NEW STRATEGY

At the time we had calculated that building an orphanage for 100 children will cost at least €100,000

That was an investment of roughly a thousand euros per child. In addition to these initial costs, we had additional costs to hire staff to care for the children. In addition, we had to buy food, clothing, medical care and other supplies, and we also had to maintain the buildings. However, if we were to buy land for €1000, it would be large enough to support one poor family who would adopt a daughter into their family. And so we saw a new better strategy that was cheaper, more family-oriented and more natural than placing the children in an orphanage.

And so our new strategy was born. We threw our nets out on the other side of the boat.

CHAPTER 6
A NEW PERSPECTIVE

So, we decided to buy land instead to build orphanages. But now, we were faced with a big challenge—convincing our sponsors that even though the strategy had changed, the vision had not. It was simply a more effective, cheaper, and natural way to meet the needs of both the poor Dalit families and the helpless and hopeless baby girls. It took some time before the board of Abba Child Care embraced the new strategy. We needed their approval before we could launch it and work with potential donors. However, in retrospect, it all went quite smoothly once we "started casting the net on the other side of the boat."

After all the struggles and setbacks surrounding Abba Village, we now saw with our own eyes that God had a much better plan in mind.

When we started on this new path, our God came to our aid in a big way. Friends of ours who run Jesus Heals and were mostly operating under the radar in Rajasthan were very happy with what we were doing for the street children in Chennai, Andhra Pradesh, Orissa, and Rajasthan.

But they were not happy with our plans for Rajasthan and urged us very earnestly not to build Abba Village.

They feared violent backlash from the Hindu community because of their belief that orphans are a curse. We had already noticed this attitude from the owners of the houses we had temporarily rented to accommodate the children.

They would rather see us leave today than tomorrow. So we took our friends to heart.

In the meantime, we were in urgent need of shelter for the 420 orphans and children who had been freed from slavery. Where should we go with them? This was our greatest concern, and we shared it with our friends of Jesus Heals.

They heard the cry of our hearts and immediately took action. As successful businessmen from Rajasthan, they knew the Christian community very well. They searched among them for families who wanted to adopt a child. To our surprise, within half a year, they found enough families to take in all 420 of our children. Now, all our children were safely in loving families, and we could leave the business to them with a clear conscience.

But they did so much more. We had already bought a large piece of land to build Abba Village, and we needed money to buy new land. So, they decided to buy our land for the full price plus a 25 percent increase so that we could acquire other pieces of land in South India to execute our new strategy. Suddenly, our plans gained momentum at an accelerated speed.

We also sold our children's home in Andhra Pradesh to a friendly Christian organization that lovingly cared for our children and even started a primary school for them. The same happened with the over 400 children we had saved after the 2008 massacre in Orissa. With that money, we bought another piece of land in Tamilnadu.

The beauty of this development was that we had found reliable Christian partners to care for our children in Rajasthan, Orissa, and Andhra-Pradesh. Also, Kingsly no longer had to divide his attention across all corners of India. Now, he could fully focus on the new developments in Tamilnadu.

So, we started looking for a suitable place to start a farm and found a beautiful plot in Uthiramerur. This district, south of Chennai, is mainly agricultural land. Later, we also bought some adjacent plots of land until we had about ten hectares of land. This is where we started to implement our new strategy. We initially called our farm the Abba Farm, although we later called it The Land of Goshen, named after the story of the Israelites who went to live in the Nile Delta of Egypt. God blessed Goshen in a special way because of His people Israel. In the same way, we felt so blessed with this beautiful farmland. The land we now call Goshen turned out to be a most blessed place indeed, as we have discovered over the years.

At the same time we bought The Land of Goshen, we contacted friends who introduced us to the "Farming God's Way" method, developed by Angus Buchan, a Christian African farmer. This method produced about 30 percent more crops than traditional farming methods in tropical countries. We started applying this method immediately and taught our Dalit families how to cultivate crops using it. If you would like to learn more about Farming God's Way, visit https:// farming-gods-way.org.

We saw the results right away. Our elephant grass grew at least 30 percent higher than our neighbors who were using traditional farming methods. The cows eating this grass produced milk that was 30 percent fattier. Even the quality of our rice was so much better because we did it God's way. The Tamilnadu State Agriculture Council inspected and saw the amazing results and high quality of our products. Because of these achievements, we even received an honorary award for our organization. However, we gave all the glory to our God. It wasn't about just being smart or having good ideas; it was God's invisible blessings that had manifested themselves. However, Kingsly and I had no idea that it was only the small beginning of something that would surpass our wildest dreams in the years to come.

CHAPTER 7

LIVING WATER FESTIVAL

We felt so blessed by the brothers of Jesus Heals Ministry. We applaud them for their tremendous help in lifting such a big burden from our shoulders. They placed these children with loving christian families, so we were greatly inspired to do the same—we developed a family-oriented plan. After all, a child needs more than a brick house and food; he or she needs a home and a warm, loving nest where they belong. Every child needs a mommy and a daddy. They need brothers and sisters and the assurance of belonging. So, we developed Abba Family Homes. Our new strategy was a double-edged sword. The poor Dalit families were themselves in need but still showed the utmost love for the poor children. Abba Family Homes would solve two needs: the needs of the Dalit families who would get a piece of land on lease and the poor children's need for love, acceptance, and care.

So, we developed the slogan: "Give a child a family and that family a future!"

Our new plan had a strong advantage over the old plan—benefits for the child, the adoptive parents, our non-profit organization, and the children's sponsors.

> ## GIVE A CHILD A FAMILY AND THAT FAMILY A FUTURE!

The child would escape a life in which misery, begging, prostitution, slavery, and early death were almost unavoidable. Instead, they would grow up in a loving family—with a mother and father and, most likely, brothers and sisters. Instead of aging out of the orphanage, they would now grow up naturally bonded to a family. Even if a child was slow to develop, they would not be thrown out because they had become part of a loving family.

The adoptive parents were previously exploited by wealthy, prominent farmers to work as slave laborers on their land for a pittance. But with our Abba Family Home program, they escape poverty and generate a decent income for their families through their own labor. In addition, they are now developing dignity and self-esteem as they break free from slavery and the poverty mentality.

As for us, our non-profit has benefited because we see each and every one of our sponsored children growing up according to God's original plan: in a family, in a household, with a father, mother, brothers and sisters!

This plan was much cheaper to implement than building an orphanage. For the same amount of money, someone could now help two children instead of one, which means that even a sponsor with a small budget can still make a big difference in the life of a helpless child. Moreover, we no longer had the task of raising these children because their foster parents lifted this burden from our shoulders—one less worry. After a child has grown up and the family can stand on their own two feet, we can reuse the land to help another family who wants to adopt a child.

We saw only amazing benefits and realized why God had redirected us from building Abba Village to building Abba Family Homes. All glory to our God for His wisdom and guidance!

After this great transition, we were launched into another, even greater plan. A new source of blessing was opened up to us—both natural and "living water."

LIVING WATER

In 2013, I invited Kingsly to visit me in the Netherlands. To promote our projects, I had organized several meetings, including a benefit dinner for entrepreneurs. Upon arrival, Kingsly immediately shared the urgent need for clean water for the poor, discriminated Dalits.

We all know that clean water is a basic need for all people. The Uthiramerur region is mainly agricultural land, which is generally owned by rich, upper-caste Hindu farmers. However, the majority of the population consists of the low-caste Dalits who work on the land of the rich, upper-caste Hindus for a meager salary. Unfortunately, they are not allowed to drink water from the wells of the rich because they are considered unclean. Those who dared to draw water from their wells are often cursed, beaten, and chased away as if they have committed a serious crime. Sometimes, they are beaten to the point of death. It is terrible and almost unimaginable for Westerners, but this is the harsh reality in large parts of India.

Dalits are forced to walk long distances to a well to get drinking water, and then they must journey back home in the burning sun with a heavy jerrycan full of clean drinking water. Because of the distance and the hard work, some drink polluted water from ponds and small lakes that is unsuitable for human consumption, and they certainly suffer the consequences. Many poor Dalits will contract water-related diseases such as dysentery and cholera. In many cases, this leads to serious illness and even death in small children, the weak, and the elderly. This was a major concern for Kingsly and the Dalit families—our primary Abba Family Home adoptive parents.

So, dreaming about providing clean drinking water for these dear people, Kingsly had a plan. Upon his arrival in the Netherlands, he shared his wish to dig two large wells, buy two tankers, and deliver the water to their villages. I did not feel good about this plan because an open well can easily become polluted. Moreover, I thought about the heavy tanker that would have to drive over the bad roads to the villages every day.

What if a well gets polluted? And what if a car breaks down? How, then, will they get their water? Isn't there a better way to provide their villages with water?

I asked Kingsly, "What do you think if we drill a pipe deep into the ground—that is, dig a well—and build a tank with taps in the middle of the village where everyone can get clean drinking water?"

"Yes, pastor" (Kingsly always calls me "pastor"). "But that would cost us almost twice as much money—about €100,000 for fifty wells in fifty villages." I remained silent for a while, looked at Kingsly thoughtfully, and then said, "It is more expensive, but if I lived in such a village, I would prefer to have the well close to home so that I could get clean drinking water anytime I wanted to. I really believe it is God's will that we do what is best for them. So let us build wells in each village so that the Dalits can pump water and tap from the storage tank."

After Kingsly and I made the final decision, I looked at my watch and said, "Quick, it's time to go to the benefit dinner we organized for Abba Child Care!"

So, we drove to the restaurant where the dinner was being held. Friends, sponsors, and various potential donors were invited. It was a cheerful and joyful gathering. Good musicians played and as the evening progressed, Kingsly shared his heart. He explained how, in India, the religious caste system causes painful discrimination against the low-ranking, casteless Dalits, commonly called "the untouchables."

I supported Kingsly and shared my heart for the Dalits, as well. Although Kingsly and I had made our plan for providing the Dalits access to clean drinking only moments ago, I changed the subject on a whim and shared our need to dig fifty wells in fifty villages, which would cost €2,000 each. "So, all together, we need €100,000 to realize this dream," I said.

After the break, a friend of mine encouraged the businessmen to invest their money in our projects so that the poorest of the poor could have their basic needs met. Then, much to our surprise, he said out of the blue, "I will invest €100,000 so that these poor people will have access to clean drinking water!"

We were stunned. We had only just launched the vision a few hours before, and God had already provided! Wow! I was ecstatic and euphoric. Other sponsors also gave donations that evening, so by the end of the evening, almost €200,000 had been donated for the projects.

Overwhelmed by the generous gifts, we went home that evening excited, our heads and hearts overwhelmed with joy and amazement.

That evening, I had a vision of a great festival and said to Kingsly, "When you go back, please dig the wells as soon as possible—before I come to India in a few months. I want to share the joy of God's provision with the villagers. Then, I would like to tell them about the "living water" of Christ, because once you drink of it, you will never be thirsty again!"

I also asked Kingsly to negotiate a big discount since we had to buy fifty pumps, fifty tanks, fifty faucets, fifty pipes, and more.

NEW POTS AND NEW HOLES

This did not fall on deaf ears. Kingsly managed to negotiate a 12.5 percent discount. With that money, we bought 10,000 water pots so that people could tap clean drinking water from these "new wells" with their "new pots." The sturdy plastic pots cannot break, and they hold about sixteen liters of water. They have a narrow neck, so they can cover the pot with a saucer to prevent dust and insects from falling in.

This sounds very primitive to Western people who all have multiple taps in their houses with clean water flowing from them.

However, for these poor Dalits, permanent access to clean drinking water was a great upgrade. Since we completed this project, almost no one has died from water-related diseases. Hallelujah!

Kingsly contacted the mayors of each village. Because they are small villages, there is only one town hall for all fifty in the regional capital, where they conducted their joint policy. Now Kingsly needed permission from the mayors to dig these fifty wells.

LIVING WATER FESTIVAL

The central government was doing nothing about the polluted water, but Kingsly managed to win the mayors' favor. To distribute the pots fairly among the poorest, Kingsly had 10,000 coupons printed. Each coupon read, "exchangeable for a free water pot." He gave each mayor 200 of these coupons to distribute among the poorest in their villages. His final request was for the mayors to transport the people to the "Living Water Festival," which was held in a field near the central town of Uthiramerur. Kingsly cleverly won the favor of the local authorities by ensuring they benefitted. By allowing the Dalits to fetch water from these wells, personally distributing the tickets, and transporting people to the festival, the authorities could win the villagers over, increasing their chances of re-election in the upcoming elections.

Their selfish motives did not bother Kingsly. All he cared about was the opportunity to talk to people about Jesus, the Living Water. Kingsly's ability to win the mayors' favor impressed me. It was clear that the Holy Spirit had guided him.

Just as the rebuilding of the walls of Jerusalem in the time of Nehemiah (Nehemiah 6:15) was completed in just fifty days, so also were the wells built within that timeframe.

The number fifty has deep biblical and prophetic significance—it points to Pentecost and the outpouring of the Holy Spirit. We had fifty villages, fifty mayors, and fifty wells in fifty days. Could we now also expect an outpouring of the Holy Spirit?

Having access to clean drinking water everywhere was an astonishing miracle that brought new hope to these Dalit villagers. When I went to India in late 2013, preparations for the Living Water Festival were already in full swing.

Not everyone was happy about it, though. So, we had to be careful how we presented ourselves. But by the grace of God and with the favor Kingsly had gained with the mayors, it all went well. Only the weather was a spoilsport. The festival was to last three days. The first day it rained, so we saw fewer people than expected. I spoke about the water available underground and how our God had answered our prayer by providing the money to bring the water from these springs to the surface so that the thirsty could drink. The shadow story of the living water is what I actually wanted to talk about, but the Lord led me to save the heartbeat of this message for the last night. The parable of the living water was clearly present in my message but hidden in the parable. Everything went smoothly.

The second day was cancelled due to heavy rain. I was disappointed, but such things happen. So, we all prayed fervently that the last day would be successful because that was the day the villagers would receive their water pot upon presentation of their receipt.

Fortunately, the weather was good on the last day, although the field was quite muddy. It did not take long before many trucks, loaded with people from all the surrounding villages, arrived and filled the field. I think we had almost ten thousand people that night together. Indians love to dance, so we had great songs, and the dancers attracted more people who passed by on the main road. By the time the dancing was over, I was asked to share my message.

Suddenly, there was a lot of commotion. Some villagers started running to the water pots, afraid that they would be too late and not get a pot. When one sheep crosses the dam, more follow, and many began to do this. It caused confusion and chaos while I was about to address the crowd.

However, our God makes all things work together for good, as my message emerged in an astonishing way from this chaos.

I took the microphone and told the people to sit down because there were enough pots for everyone. Instead, the villagers were to pick up their pots at the end of the meeting in an orderly manner. Fortunately, the stewards helped direct people back to their seats.

I asked the villagers to take their seats and warned then that if we don't listen, we can't hear anything, and if we can't hear, we can't have faith, for faith comes by hearing.

Suddenly, the message was crystal clear in my mind as I repeated, "Sit down and listen, for you must listen to hear, and hear to believe, and believe to receive!"

A hush fell over the audience, and attention was now focused on the stage. I repeated:

"There are three steps you have to take:

1) You must listen to hear

2) You must hear to believe

3) You must believe to receive!"

I picked up a one-thousand-rupee note, waved it in the air, and said, "Listen, I am going to give this thousand-rupee note to the first person who comes forward when I say so! Now, if you don't listen, you don't hear, and if you don't hear, how can you believe? So listen! If you hear me, you must believe me—I am not lying or trying to deceive you. If you do not believe me, you will certainly not be blessed. So, you must believe me, but even believing is not enough because faith without works is dead. If you believe me, you must also come to receive what I have promised."

The audience was spellbound. Some wondered if I was joking or serious. Then I said, "I see that you are listening, and also that you hear me, and some believe me too. But now it is time to translate your trust into action. The first one to come forward will get this one-thousand-rupee note."

Many seemed to wonder if this white man was playing a game with them. But then a little boy came forward. I think he was barely six years old. Suddenly, the rest of the people woke up, and others started running too, many catching up with the little boy. But the little boy made it first, so I pulled him up on the high platform and handed him the note. He was a little shy but smiled happily. Then, I said to the crowd, "You see? You must become like a child: simply hear, believe, come and receive the blessing of God!"

I continued: "Unfortunately, I cannot give you all one thousand rupees, but I did not lie. And God did not lie. As an ambassador of the Most High, I prayed to Him to provide you with clean drinking water, and He answered our prayer. He has provided you with this clean water that will not make you sick!"

"But our God has even better water. A water that, if you drink it, you will never be thirsty again. That is the Living Water. And if you drink it, it will cleanse your innermost being. It will wash away all the filth from your life, and you will never be thirsty again!"

"I did not lie about the springs of water, and I did not lie about the thousand rupees, and I also did not lie about this Living Water that will cleanse your soul from sin. If you want to drink this water, I invite you in the name of the Lord Jesus to come and drink it for free! You have heard me, you have believed me, and now it is time to come and receive it. Just come … come … come!"

Suddenly, the whole crowd ran to the platform. Never before had I seen such a response to a call. At first, I did not know what to do, but then I felt that I had to lay my hands on them and bless them in the name of Jesus. Our whole team was called forward to lay hands on the people. The people were extremely motivated to be blessed and touched. There was such a desire, such a hunger, such an urge that they almost pushed each other to be blessed. In fact, people were almost fighting with each other to pull my arm and hand onto their heads. They were crying, and I could see tears streaming down their faces. They looked like little children begging and climbing onto daddy's lap for a hug. It overwhelmed me to see such intense reactions. We didn't even have time to say long prayers, as so many people were looking to me for a touch from God and to enjoy the Living Water.

When the prayers were almost over, people came forward with their receipts to receive their water pots. It was such a colorful scene—all these Indians in their colorful saris receiving their multi-colored pots.

SHEEP WITHOUT A SHEPHERD

As the pots were exchanged for their tokens from the stage, I stepped back to view the colorful scene. As I thought about what had just happened, the Holy Spirit began to speak to me: "Do they know what they have done? Do they realize who Christ, the Giver of Living Water, is? How can we help them further in their newfound faith? Is there a church in their village? Is there a shepherd who can lead them to green pastures? What if there is no one and the devil comes to steal the seed that was sown tonight?"

I was rudely awakened from this moment of contemplation. Suddenly, I realized that we would have to build churches in these villages and look for shepherds and pastors to disciple these new believers. These people did not know anything yet. I walked over to Kingsly and asked, "How much would it cost to build a small church in each village and dig a well next to them?" Kingsly replied with €20,000. Kingsly looked at me questioningly, but before Kingsly could say anything else, I said, "Then we will build fifty churches—one in each village!"

A new vision was born!

CHAPTER 8

A CHURCH IN EVERY VILLAGE

After this beautiful meeting, where God had moved so miraculously, we were all ecstatic about the power and presence of God and the hungry response of the people who were fighting to get our hands on their heads. So I asked John, Kingsly's father, "Why are they fighting to get my hand on their heads? I don't understand."

John explained: "Remember, they are Dalits, which means they are 'untouchables.' No one is allowed to touch them because they are considered unclean. A Hindu or a Brahmin of a high caste doesn't even want a shadow of a Dalit to fall on him or on his clothes. But now you have come to teach them that they can be children of the Most High, children of the King of kings. And you gently, lovingly, graciously laid your hands on them. You have no idea what that means to them. To them, it is as if God Himself is touching them. That is what these simple people believe. Finally, they are no longer 'untouchables' because the servant of the Most High God has touched them with a healing and blessed touch!"

I cried when I heard John explain what had happened that evening at the Living Water Festival. How were these precious people deprived of God's loving touch for so long? And what did they really understand about the message—of God's love and the sacrifice of His Son? Almost nothing!

How then would they survive, thrive, and grow in their newfound faith?

I knew that we must indeed do something. We must build churches and train and equip pastors and teachers to help these new believers grow in knowing the living and loving God whose hands were pierced for the lepers and laid on these "untouchables." My vision to build fifty churches became a plan of action that same night. I was determined to put my hand to the plough and not look back. But this was easier said than done.

When I got home, I shared my vision with others, not yet knowing where the supply would come from. There were many dubious and serious looks and a lot of questions.

"How are you going to do that?"

"I don't know!"

"Where will you get the money from?"

"Well, I don't know!"

"When are you going to do it?"

"As soon as possible!"

"Who are you going to do it with?"

"I'm definitely going to do it with Kingsly!"

"How long will it take?"

"I don't know yet, but it will happen!"

"But you are an evangelist, aren't you?"

"Sure, but that doesn't matter, does it?"

Despite the critical questions, the concerned looks, and the doubtful comments about this seemingly impossible plan, nothing and no one could stop me.

> # IF THIS PLAN FAILED, IT WOULD BE MY FAULT, BUT IF IT SUCCEEDED, IT WOULD BE TO GOD'S GLORY!

When they told me I was crazy, I responded, "Yes, I am crazy . . . crazy about Jesus!"

As time went by, churches, businesspeople, individuals, and companies began to believe in my dream. Slowly but surely, support came from all sides. Yes, even from people whom we least expected. But yet another miracle was needed. What do you do with churches who have pastors who cannot provide the necessary care for these new believers? So, we prayed not only for the money to build the churches but also for leaders who could build up the people. In a special way, God also provided this need.

In March 2014, we launched our plan for fifty multifunctional village halls, and in May of that same year, three were fully sponsored, and another seven pledged. New villages were found, and money kept coming in. God blessed and provided the necessary funds. In January 2015, we opened the first three churches with great enthusiasm, and by the end of 2015, we had completed the first ten churches.

During the festive opening of the first ten churches, we saw many people come to Jesus, which called for a double celebration, on earth and in heaven. The number of adopted children had also grown to 234.

Our wild plans had suddenly seemed to take flight. As we preached Christ and taught God's Word, built our village churches and wells, cared for orphans and widows, cared for lepers, provided medical care, and started schools in our village churches for children, we prayed that God would provide the means to continue. I felt that I had now come to the center of God's will for my life.

Both Kingsly and I experienced exuberant joy and fulfillment in doing the will of our Heavenly Father as we saw these villages changed, people saved, violence decreased, and blessings increased.

PERSECUTION

However, we were not so lucky in every village. We had set our sights on Elanagar, a village in the region where we had also started building a small church. But on the night of September 11, some men came and damaged the foundation, tore down some walls, and stole building materials. They also dumped waste in the new borehole for the water tank. They attacked our guard, breaking his leg. His night shelter was also destroyed. Due to the continued attacks, we reported the matter to the police. But instead of helping us, they took Pastor Daniel into custody and blamed him for causing this misery. On September 26, 2015, he was released on bail after paying a ransom.

His family was happy that he was finally home again.

Pastor Daniel was a very faithful and prayerful man. It had been his prayer for years that there would be a house of God in his village. He saw in building of the church the fulfillment of his long-cherished desire to have his own place of worship. On Sunday, September 27, the day after his release, Pastor Daniel went to the construction site to assess the situation and pray for the completion of their future church.

Suddenly, four young men on motorbikes entered the premises. They had iron bars with them and began to beat Daniel horribly. Although some saw it and heard his cries for help, no one came to his aid. He was also stabbed in the stomach and chest. Although some bystanders witnessed the attack, help came too late as our dear friend, Pastor Daniel, died on the spot. It sent shockwaves through the community of Elanagar when this sad news came out while the local police carried away his body.

Fortunately, most of the villagers stood behind Beula, Pastor Daniel's wife, to support and comfort her and their three young daughters through this great loss. An official gathering was planned to commemorate the life of Pastor Daniel, which over a thousand people attended to show their support.

During this meeting, Beula publicly expressed her forgiveness of the perpetrators who had so cruelly murdered her beloved husband. So now, we had a widow to care for.

We hoped that over time, the tension would decrease and that we could resume construction, but the authorities did not give permission for fear of another attack. However, we kept praying that we would be able to complete this project one day. That would also be a fitting tribute to the precious blood that this martyr shed for Christ. On October 2, 2015, we buried Daniel. To date, the perpetrators have not been found.

After Pastor Daniel's funeral, Kingsly led a delegation of Christian leaders to the Governor of Tamilnadu to plead for justice, handing over a petition with over 500 Christians' signatures—an explicit plea for justice, not revenge. Afterwards, our pastors made a collective statement that our message is a message of love and forgiveness, quoting Galatians 2:20 (ESV) and Philippians 1:21 (ESV):

> *I have been crucified with Christ. It is no longer I who live, but Christ who lives in me. And the life I now live in the flesh I live by faith in the Son of God, who loved me and gave himself for me.*

> *"For to me to live is Christ, and to die is gain."*

Although the governor promised to take our petition seriously, we felt that our prayers were still much more important. Our project won tens of thousands of people who had been trapped in spiritual darkness and slavery in the demonic caste system for over 4,000 years. The devil was losing his grip on these dear people who were now getting to know their Savior and Redeemer, Jesus Christ. We saw the murder of our dear Pastor Daniel as a clear counterattack by the kingdom of darkness.

Our struggle is not against flesh and blood, but against the devil who has these precious souls bound and paralyzed by fear. But the love of our God casts out fear and sets them free.

That we survived the devil's deadly attack was nice, but we were not satisfied with that. That wasn't good enough! We resisted a counterattack by preaching the good news more and more . We would not allow the devil to intimidate and paralyze us with fear because millions of precious souls need to hear this good news. Therefore, we dis not look back; we put our hand to the plough, and we went forward courageously with determination, wisdom, courage, and perseverance.

I am so proud of our dear Indian brothers. I admire their grit, courage and determination. Most of them are simple men, mostly from very humble backgrounds. But they have shown such courage, love, and passion for Jesus, standing with their feet in the rich clay of life's trenches, on the battlefield for dear souls. They deserve our respect as living examples of following Christ. It is not about intellect, knowledge, and information, but about character!

May they all be a great inspiration to the younger generation who follows them as they follow Christ.

Although we went forward boldly, we decided to be wise and build the surrounding walls before we built a new church.

According to Indian law, crossing that wall would be a trespass on someone else's property. It would be harder to break in and a little easier to prove that our rights were violated. The setback in Elanagar and the death of Pastor Daniel have given us a full and fresh awareness that we are in a spiritual battle for precious souls for which Jesus died. However, none of our pastors and friends backed down out of fear. On the contrary, they were even more determined to preach Jesus Christ, the only hope for this dead and dying world. With more fervor and passion, they made their faces hard as flint to proclaim the message of hope and salvation.

We are indeed so proud of these simple but faithful shepherds who were willing to pay a price for preaching Christ, who paid the ultimate price to redeem us all from the power of sin forever.

CHAPTER 9

FROM DEMOLITION TO CONSTRUCTION

Another amazing story is that of the man who persecuted the church until Jesus arrested him. His name is Cittibabu, and he lived in Karuvempampoondi village with his wife and two daughters. Only afterwards did I discover that he also played a role in the great miracle that God performed in his life. Every meeting with Cittibabu is a celebration, especially when I think back to everything that preceded this great miracle.

His story is similar to the story of Paul.

About twenty years ago, Cittibabu heard the gospel for the first time, but he didn't like it. On the contrary, he hated Christians. But he also had another problem: he was using drugs, and his addiction was dominating his life more and more. His marriage suffered so much from his addiction that his wife saw no other way out than to leave him. In his loneliness, he joined a gang. In order to rise in rank and prestige among the other gang members, he had to do something "heroic." Thus, a plan was born to destroy the Christian church building in his village with a bulldozer. Driven by his hatred, he put his plan into action. He arranged for a bulldozer and razed the church building to the ground. When the pastor protested against this evil plan, they beat him half to death to silence him. But these atrocities did not alleviate his loneliness. On the contrary, it only made it worse.

To make matters worse, he had a serious accident that shattered his left leg. All he could do now was lie flat on his back and stare at the ceiling. He was desperate and thought about suicide. This was right around the time we were organizing the Living Water Festival.

When he saw the poster for this festival, he thought back to how he had rejected the gospel.

"Could this be the answer to my problem?" he asked himself. He decided to give it a try. *If it doesn't help, it doesn't hurt!* he must have thought. So, he dragged himself to the festival, heard the message of God's love and forgiveness, came forward, and gave his life to Jesus. But much more happened than he expected. Not only did he open his heart to the God of the Bible and drink the Living Water, but to his surprise, his broken leg was healed. He could walk normally again . . . what a miracle! The change in his life gave his wife confidence in their future, and so after a while, his marriage was restored.

Wow!

FROM BREAKER TO BUILDER

Grateful for the miracle that God had performed, Cittibabu wanted to give something back to Him. When he heard that we wanted to build more multifunctional village halls, he wanted to help us find good plots. After all, as a local resident, he knew the area like the back of his hand. He even wanted to help with the construction. At first, Kingsly was suspicious. *What does this man actually want from us?* he thought. Kingsly explained to Cittibabu that he had been saved by grace and that he could not buy his salvation with good works. Cittibabu understood this very well but asked in tears if he could help anyway.

He was so thankful for the miracle that God had done—not only in his body but also in his heart. He was grateful that his relationships with his wife and children had been restored. Then it dawned on Kingsly that God had done an amazing miracle in the life of this addicted, suicidal, depressed, and sick man, so he gave Cittibabu the freedom to search for a piece of land in his village to build a multifunctional community center.

What we didn't know at the time was that Cittibabu had set his sights on the site where he had destroyed the old church. And so, with Cittibabu's help, a brand-new church was built on the same site where the old one had been demolished. God works in mysterious ways, indeed! Cittibabu is now a faithful and dedicated leader and pillar of strength in the same church he once destroyed. He is also very active in the beautiful work that Abba Child Care does in that territory. Is this not the special characteristic of God's inimitable goodness and grace?

When I preached the gospel at the Living Water Festival and saw thousands of people rushing forward to accept Jesus, I had no idea of the miracle God was going to do in Cittibabu's life. In fact, I didn't know him at all. I didn't even know he existed. But God saw him in that mass of people and performed a mighty miracle in his life. It was not until a year later, after I visited India again, that I heard the remarkable story of what God had done for him.

I remember saying, "With God I rejoice over this prodigal son, who was once dead but is now alive again!"

Every time I meet with Cittibabu, he cries tears of joy and gratitude for what God has done in his life. He is so thankful for his new life, his healing, the restoration of his marriage, and the realization of God's love and forgiveness.

His eyes sparkle and shine with joy and gratitude every time he sees me, and it encourages me greatly that my labor has not been in vain. It has been worth all the effort, pain, and struggle, and I would do it again, especially considering the amazing changes we have seen in the lives of those we have reached with the good news.

Because that is, after all, the heartbeat of Abba Child Care.

WE WERE THE ANSWER TO THEIR NEEDS, AND THEY WERE THE ANSWER TO OUR NEEDS

It was amazing to see how God led us from one village to another to build even more multifunctional village halls. We also prayed fervently that God would provide us with spiritual fathers, pastors, and workers who could care for these new believers. What we didn't know is that God had already prepared the answer to our prayers. Pastors in that area had been praying for a church building of their own, which they really couldn't afford, and we were praying for pastors and leaders who could take care of that. We were the answer to their needs, and they were the answer to our needs. So, the Lord brought us together.

When we first entered Uthiramerur, we knew no one. It was an undeveloped agricultural area where many had never heard the gospel. There was a lot of spiritual darkness at first—they didn't exactly roll out the red carpet for us. But when we look back now, we see God's special hand because we have made so many good friends and found so many faithful colleagues—precious friends who have only become dearer to us over the years.

All their stories are special and remarkable. We will need eternity to tell them all. However, we can only tell a few—starting with the astonishing story of Mr. Murthy, the mayor of his village.

CHAPTER 10

THE MAYOR OF MARUTHAM

Slowly but surely, we started building our churches, but not all at once. We called them multifunctional village halls because that is what they are—we use them not only as churches but also as gathering places for the farmers, where the women can fetch water from the well.

During the week, we use them as a school for the children in the village because otherwise, most of them would never receive an education at all. It is our wish to offer education and give these children the chance to develop themselves. In the evenings, we give sewing lessons to the women in the village.

We also organize evenings where we teach about hygiene, family planning, medical care, family values, child rearing, farming methods, etc. On Sundays, we use the building as a church, and we also use it as a shelter during cyclones and as a storage facility.

By using the building in this way, we can provide a wide range of services in a very cost-effective manner for the local community. We apply these disciplines from a Christian and biblical perspective. All children, women, and men in the village are welcome to use these facilities without distinction.

When we have a village in mind to build a church, the protocol is to first contact the local authorities—that is, the mayor of the village. Without his permission, there is little we can do. So, when we had conceived the idea of building a church in Marutham, Kingsly went to visit Mr. Murthy, the mayor of his village. Mr. Murthy was receptive because he knew the whole village could benefit from our services. However, at the end of the first conversation, he asked Kingsly to pray for him. When Kingsly asked what he should pray for, Mr. Murthy told him that he had a tumor in his nose and that the doctors did not want to operate on him for fear of damaging his brain. The operation would only make his condition worse. After hearing this, Kingsly prayed a simple prayer and left Mr. Murthy.

In the weeks that followed, Mr. Murthy sneezed a lot and had blood clots coming out of his nose. At first, he had no idea that God was healing him until he went back to the doctor for a consultation. After a thorough examination, the doctor said that he could not find any trace of the cancer. Delighted with his healing, he realized that it was Kingsly's God who was behind this amazing miracle. He was so happy and thankful that he realized that we serve a living God, so he gave his life to Jesus. His wife and children immediately followed him when they witnessed the miracle God had done.

Wherever he went, the mayor enthusiastically testified to the miracle of his healing. As a result, more than six families in his village gave their lives to Christ. Before the church was completed, more and more people came to Christ. It seemed that as the building neared completion, the Christian community simultaneously grew to fill the new church building. Therefore, we earnestly prayed that a pastor would be brought in to care for the new believers.

At that time, we did not know that God had already prepared a man to fulfill this role. He had prayed for years for revival in his village and a place where they could come together to worship God. God had answered both of our prayers by bringing us together.

I also happened to be in India for the opening of the church in Marutham. The new pastor testified with tears in his eyes about how God had beautifully met both of our needs. Marutham would certainly never be the same again!

When Mr. Murthy's son, Settu, saw that God had healed his father, he also gave his life to Jesus like the rest of his family had. He has since worked for us as a supervisor of our construction project. At the opening of each new multifunctional church, Settu and his father were present, and every time, Mayor Murthy made a passionate plea—always testifying to his healing miracle—to the mayors of other villages to invite us to build a multifunctional hall in their village. We could not have imagined a better recommendation for our project. Mr. Murthy touched the hearts of other mayors to receive us as a blessing from God. In this way, many villages opened up to us.

As Mr. Murthy is a highly respected man in the council of mayors, his words were not taken lightly when he openly testified of his miraculous healing and how much of a blessing we were to all the people of his village. Initially, many of these Hindu mayors were reserved towards us as a Christian organization. But after we had dug those fifty wells to provide clean drinking water to their villages and given ten thousand water pots to the poorest of the poor, their distrust began to crumble.

Mayor Murthy's enthusiastic testimony was the final push for many mayors to invite us to build in their village.

You know the saying, "Once one sheep has jumped the dam, more will follow"? Mr. Murthy was the one sheep who set a good example and opened the floodgates. With his son Settu, the lead supervisor of the project, we gained more and more favor with the local villagers. Mr. Murthy is now a dear brother and a good friend of our work in the district Uthiramerur.

CHAPTER 11

THE CRITICAL CYCLONE SEASON

Until 2015, I had always visited India in the month of November. Although I had no real reason to postpone my visit until January 2016, it ended up being a good decision because in November 2015, Tamilnadu was hit by mega cyclone Michaung.

The monsoon rains were extremely heavy and caused widespread flooding in southern India. Chennai and its surrounding districts were hit the worst.

It rained incessantly for over two weeks, and Chennai received even more rain than expected. According to the weather report, the water level in Chennai reached the highest level ever recorded in history. More than 500 people were killed and over 1.8 million were displaced. With damage and loss estimates ranging from $2 billion to $1 trillion, this cyclone was the most expensive to date.

The floods in the city of Chennai were described as the worst in a century. Chennai was officially declared a disaster area. Officials of the Chennai Corporation said that at least 57,000 homes in the city suffered structural damage, especially those of the working class. More than 3 million families suffered total or partial damage to their homes, and nearly 100,000 livestock and many poultry were drowned.

Even the large jumbo jets at Chennai International Airport were up to their hulls in water. Take-off, flying, and landing were absolutely impossible. I would have been unable to land in Chennai if I had planned to travel in November.

MEGA CYCLONE MICHAUNG IN 2015

So, we thanked God that we had decided go in January 2016 instead.

The rain in Chennai caused large parts of the city to be flooded. This was especially because of the inadequate drainage system in the city. It could not handle the excess water, which caused enormous damage to houses—especially the small mud huts of the Dalit population. They recorded 1,185 millimeters of rain in Chennai in less than fourteen days. This was a record-breaking flood, which reached a maximum of 1,088 millimeters. As a result of the rain, water reservoirs and lakes filled up. Flights were canceled, trains were delayed, and bus services were canceled as roads and airports were flooded. Parts of the city were inaccessible, and people drowned as a result of fallen power poles and collapsed roofs, walls, and houses. Many churches also stood under water, some up to a height of almost two meters.

The government and many NGOs did their best to help. Slums, in particular, were flooded, forcing residents to flee from the growing water levels, leaving their meager shelter behind to later discover all their possessions had been washed away. For many, cows and goats are the only source of income, and much of their livestock drowned because they were unable to save them.

All this led to great fear and uncertainty about their future. The most vulnerable groups were small children and the elderly. Many suffered from hunger and lacked proper sanitation. People stayed in bus stations, schools, churches, and temples on higher ground to stay away from the water. Most of the time, clean water supplies were also contaminated during such floods.

The irony of these floods is that people are drowning in water while dying of thirst because they don't have access to clean drinking water. So, many contract water-transmitted diseases, such as dysentery, because they have no choice but to drink contaminated water.

In addition, finding food is a big challenge for the affected people because government aid cannot reach everyone.

Mega cyclone Michaung affected the poorest of the poor—the Dalits—in particular. Their only hope was now lost, and they feared for their lives, as the little they had built up over the years was gone in one fell swoop. Their lives were wiped out by this disaster, along with their hopes for a better life. Who would help these people?

Doing nothing was not an option. When I learned of this devastating news, I felt I had to do something. Although Abba Child Care was not developed to meet the needs of disaster victims, Kingsly and I did not hesitate to do our utmost to help the victims as best we could. So, in a brainstorming session, we decided to put together a survival kit for families, which we called a "Hope Box."

HOPE BOX PROJECT

While I sent €5,000 to buy the ingredients for the Hope Boxes, I also sent out a newsletter to raise more money to meet this urgent need.

Meanwhile, Kingsly ordered large quantities of basic necessities such as food, medicine, clothing, and shelter. The Hope Boxes included a hot meal, clean water, bread, and blankets. We chose to include rice, sugar, salt, oil, wheat, cookies, a jerry can for clean drinking water, detergent, soap, blankets, sleeping mats, cooking utensils for a small family, medicines, and powdered milk in each Hope Box. One box would last a month for a family of four, making a huge difference in the lives of many who would otherwise die. This small token of love brought back a little joy and a smile to the faces of those who had lost everything.

The contents of one box cost €25, which is actually a small amount, considering the glimmer of hope it could offer a whole family in such a hopeless situation. We were able to gather thousands of families and provide them with a Hope Box, and many sponsors responded to the call to donate one or more of them.

Many of the sponsors knew about our agricultural project, so they also asked how our people in the countryside were doing. They wanted to know if our adoptive parents survived the flood and whether they lost their homes or livestock.

I was worried about these questions, but Kingsly fortunately brought us good news. Even though the surrounding areas were badly affected by the flood, we were not. He reminded me that we had named our farm "The Land of Goshen" after the place where the people of Israel lived during their exile in Egypt and that many of the ten plagues had passed the land of Goshen by. It seemed we were divinely protected, as this cyclone barely touched our people or our farm. Not one of our animals had drowned. On the contrary, while the thunder rolled and the lightning struck, many of our goats had given birth, even to twins. We had literally seen the hand of God's protection on our projects, so we used our money to help the victims elsewhere.

Many victims received their boxes with great gratitude and asked who we were and why we were doing it. This gave us a golden opportunity to tell them about the love of Jesus and how He had inspired us to do the possible while we saw Him do the impossible when he sent us more sponsors.

CYCLONE NIVAR IN 2017

Monsoon season seems to be almost an annual disaster for South India.

Nowadays, it is a rare exception for a cyclone not to hit Chennai, and in November 2017, Cyclone Nivar hit Chennai.

Tens of thousands of people lost their homes, which are usually nothing more than a simple hut. We immediately started another Hope Box campaign, but we changed the name to Hope Bag because a bag is easier to carry.

> **BRING HOPE TO THE HOPELESS, LOVE TO THE LOVELESS, AND LIFE TO THE LIFELESS.**

However, the contents were the same—a one-month supply for a family of four. We were able to help over 2,000 families affected by Cyclone Nivar. We thought about how much we would cry out for help if we were in their shoes. We identified with them, which motivated us to extend a helping hand and share our blessings with them. This is when our organization, Sharing Hands, was born. We lived up to the name; we always have, and we always will, for as long as we can. Our motto has always been and will always be: "May God help us to be an extension of His loving, pierced hands to bring hope to the hopeless, love to the loveless, and life to the lifeless.

CYCLONE GAJA IN 2018

At the end of November 2018, it happened again, and Cyclone Gaja powerfully hit our area. Over a hundred thousand people lost their homes. At least thirty-five people died in the storm when their shaky homes were blown away. Trees were uprooted, people and livestock drowned, causing a lot of damage and chaos.

I immediately transferred ten thousand euros to start first aid for the victims. Once again, our farm and our farmers were spared this time. Was this coincidence or divine providence? We do not know, but we heard the cries of the victims and took action to help as much as possible.

Who knows, we thought, *maybe next time, we'll be hit!*

CYCLONE BOB-06

Indeed, less than a year later, our area was hit by another cyclone—Bob-06. Initially, we didn't know how bad this cyclone would be, but it didn't take long to realize that it was even worse than Cyclone Michaung, and this time, we would not be spared—not because the cyclone hit us so hard but because the government wanted to spare other areas that had been hit hard earlier. Therefore, they opened the floodgates to let the water flow freely into our agricultural area. Many of our adoptive families, widows, and lepers were badly affected by this flood. Three widows died of hypothermia when their villages were up to their knees in water. We were angry and frustrated that the government did this without consulting any of the residents. Maybe they had no other choice.

We were also worried that if the water level remained this high, we would lose our crops. This flood was worse than the 2015 flood and exceeded all recorded floods in the history of this region.

As a result, all the water reservoirs and lakes were full. No plane could land, trains were delayed, and buses were at a standstill because the roads were flooded. Some areas were inaccessible, and people died under collapsing roofs, walls, and washed away houses. Others died when electricity pylons fell in the water. Many of our churches in the areas of Uthiramerur, Chengalpattu, and Cheyyur were also submerged. Many of our goats and cows drowned. It seemed like our life's work had been irreparably affected, and we feared for the future of our adoptive parents and farmers. Young children and the elderly were the most vulnerable, as many lacked adequate sanitation. Most fled to higher ground and sought shelter in temples, schools, bus stations, churches, and other public buildings.

After these cyclones, we usually see an outbreak of dysentery, diarrhea, cholera, and other waterborne diseases. And then there is the struggle for food, and the poorest people, the Dalits, are the biggest victims of these circumstances. Their only hope was lost, and they feared for their lives as their meager means of sustenance were gone overnight, along with their hope for a better future.

It was time for action again. We had no time to lose. We had just received ten new gospel trucks. (We will tell you more about these wonderful tools in chapter 19.) We immediately drove them to the disaster area to bring food, clothing, medicine, water, tents, and other supplies. At the same time, we evacuated the people to a safe place on higher ground. It was the best start to use these trucks to save people in their distress. We again deployed the Hope Bag project and immediately sent € 200,000. In addition, we asked our friends and sponsors to support us. Over time, we were able to help more than 10,000 families with a Hope Bag.

OPERATION RESTORATION

After the water had subsided for a while, we assessed the damage the cyclone had caused. Our adoptive parents and farmers had lost 280 cows. I won't even mention the loss of their homes and other things but when a small farmer loses his cattle, he loses his hope. It was heartbreaking and devastating; however, we wanted to restore and rebuild hope. So, we started "Operation Restoration." And then God did another amazing miracle.

One of our mystery sponsors heard about the disaster and opened both his heart and his wallet. He wanted to encourage each of these families by sending us enough money to help buy each family a cow. Altogether, we bought 280 cows. Wow, what a miracle! And what's more, we discovered that many of these cows were pregnant. Within a short time, each cow had a calf, and now, they had milk, and more than that—they had hope again!

Kingsly has collected and filed the stories of all the affected families. Each family received a cow, and each story is a testimony of hope, grace, and gratitude. With this selfless act of compassion and kindness, more than just a cow was released—new hope was, too—hope for tomorrow, hope for the future, and hope in God! If you are interested and want to read these stories, you can scan the QR code or visit https://www.abbachildcare.org/uploads/7/8/2/6/7826556/farmerscows2.pdf.

Although this disaster sidetracked us, we felt we were on God's track. Remarkably, this disaster had no negative impact on our other projects—on the contrary!

Because we put God first, He opened His unlimited resources and provided sufficient means to do all that He had called us to do.

Since this disaster, we have been involved in another flood disaster in Himachal Pradesh, Northern India. Many dear people died, and entire villages were washed away.

> **WE HAVE DISTRIBUTED NOT ONLY BREAD AND WATER BUT ALSO THE BREAD OF LIFE AND THE LIVING WATER.**

A missionary friend of ours was working in this area, so we couldn't resist taking money out of our budget and sending him €60,000 to distribute Hope Bags to the victims. You can read the full story here: https://www.abbachildcare. org/uploads/7/8/2/6/7826556/hulpverlening_ bij_de_overvloeden_in_himachal_pradesh_ by_abba.copy.pdf.

To express our commitment, we have distributed not only bread and water but also the bread of life and the Living Water.

However, we endured yet another disaster—not a natural disaster but a terrible bloodbath in North East India in the state of Manipur—the violent persecution of the Kuki tribe. We can't say too much about it, but if you're interested, you can read the whole story (in English) here: https://www.abba- childcare.org/uploads/7/8/2/6/7826556/abba_ outreach_in_manipur.pdf.

These additional projects in aiding natural disasters and persecution did not deter us from our initial call to preach Christ and care for the orphans and widows. On the contrary, our work during these disasters gave us hundreds of golden opportunities to share the love of God with the victims. We found so many open, receptive, and responsive hearts from even the simplest acts, like giving them a cup of water and a piece of bread. They recognized the loving and caring hand of God in small gestures of care and concern, and because of that, we were able to quench their deepest thirst for the Living Water and satisfy their hunger for the bread of life: Jesus Christ.

CHAPTER 12
CHARITY DINNERS

A lot of money is needed to sponsor our farmland projects, the multi-functional churches, and the orphans and widows. I founded Abba Child Care as an NGO to channel the funds and donations of friends and donors who so generously want to invest in our work. Through the website, news updates, promo movies, and presentations on social media, I did my utmost to present and share the projects we had been working on.

My wife, Antje, who was born in the Netherlands to Indonesian parents, supported me with all her heart. Although she was not involved in the administration, registration, or presentation of the projects, she was fully involved in her husband's work with all her heart and soul.

Antje has a unique talent for cooking, especially when it comes to Indonesian food. She inherited that gift from her lovely mother, who was also an excellent cook. I enjoy her Indonesian and Moluccan dishes like no other. Because cooking is her passion and her life, she finds great satisfaction in cooking for others.

Even though Antje is not a speaker or organizer, she has still found a way to contribute with her talent. I truly believe that we all have talents that can be used for the glory of God. By using your talent, you kill two birds with one stone. We have used Antje's cooking skills to organize benefit dinners. The guests will experience a wonderful evening with an exotic Indonesian dinner, supplemented with speeches and presentations about our projects. We are always happy to present our work and get in touch with potential sponsors. Our projects reap the benefits of these events in the form of donations to realize the vision.

Antje thought about what else she could do to support the work, and she came up with the idea to cook and sell Indonesian food for the charity projects of Abba Child Care. So, a new vision and mission were born.

Over time, we have held several successful charity events, raising a lot of sponsorship money. At one of these events, we invited Kingsly to come to the Netherlands to share our story from his perspective with our friends and sponsors.

For Kingsly, a benefit dinner was a brand-new way to present our work. India holds very few, if any, charity dinners, but he liked it so much that he suggested organizing a benefit dinner in India as well. So, he invited Antje and me to come to India, cook an Indonesian meal, and encourage the Indian people to sponsor projects at a benefit dinner.

We didn't know whether it would catch on in Indian culture, but if you don't shoot, you'll never hit. That's why we decided to first try it out and see if it would catch on. So, we started advertising it. Initially, not too many people responded. To get people in, Kingsly's father lowered the price of the tickets to less than the cost of the ingredients. Still, we didn't get many responses. Kingsly's father took it a step further and invited a lot of people to come for free. Before we knew it, there were 200 visitors on the list, which then grew to 250 and then to over 300. Wow! Antje had never cooked for so many people before.

Together with Kingsly's wife, Anita, we calculated how much vegetables, meat, herbs, rice, garlic, onions, ginger, and other spices we needed. I love making big bowls of sambal (a spicy Indonesian pepper sauce) to spice up the food a bit because Indians generally like their food really spicy.

Antje got help from Anita and a large group of ladies to cut the vegetables. The pots they used were so big that you could easily boil a goat in them. They stirred the pot with a spoon that was almost two meters long. You really needed muscles to stir the contents in the pot. Thank God for their local cook, a strong man who knew how to cook in these big pots. These huge pots were heated with firewood. It was a great sight to see this small Indonesian lady cooking in this traditional way. Soon, the smell of the dish filled the room, and our mouths started to water.

Although I was used to this kind of Indonesian food, I realized that most Indians had never eaten Indonesian food, and certainly not the specific taste of the island of Ambon. Most Indians eat a lot of rice and almost no vegetables. Now it was the other way around with this delicious Indonesian food. Fortunately, they all liked her food. Some even came for a second plate, and by the end, all the food was gone.

> # SHARING THE VISION UNITED OUR HEARTS TO WORK TOGETHER, MAKING EVERYONE JOYFULLY WANT TO CONTRIBUTE THEIR SHARE.

Kingsly and I shared the vision of our projects, and although we did not expect much from the poor people, it was amazing to discover that together they had sponsored almost a complete multifunctional village church. The next day, some business friends promised to contribute. One through sponsoring the cement, another wanted to supply the bricks, and a third took care of the window frames. In the end, it was a great success.

Eating together and sharing the vision united our hearts to work together, making everyone joyfully want to contribute their share.

I was very proud. After all, most of the fundraising came from the Netherlands. But now I saw with my own eyes how the relatively poor local population was committed to raising money for their own church. That made me feel proud of my Indian friends. Because they had now given from the little they had, they now also become candidates to receive, because what you sow, you will reap!

A few years later, we had another charity dinner in India. This time, Antje cooked for almost 400 people. She and Anita, who had become her best friend, filled the plates for every visitor with great pleasure. It was a wonderful sight for Kingsly and me to see our wives so happy and working together for the benefit of the projects that God had entrusted to us. Tears of joy and gratitude flowed abundantly as we felt God's amazing presence and experienced His mighty blessing.

We looked forward to the future with joy and excitement, as we felt that God had many more blessings in store for us as we sought to do His will.

CHAPTER 13
THE LAND OF GOSHEN

As I mentioned earlier, we named our first farm The Land of Goshen, and after the big cyclone of 2015, we were fortunate to have been passed by without any damage. On the contrary, we were blessed with new life, twin goats, and great harvests beyond our expectations.

Although this was partly due to the way we worked the land, Kingsly and I believe this blessing was mainly due to God's mighty hand on their work.

In Marudham, Mayor Murthy's village, where we built one of our first multi-purpose village houses, the church had grown to over a hundred members. Not a single crime has been recorded in Marudham since their church was built in 2015. Even the secular authorities noticed this and rewarded the church for its positive influence in creating a peaceful atmosphere in Marudham. However, we know that it is God's blessing and not so much the result of our efforts. In the same way, we saw the blessing on our farm, where our elephant grass grows more than a foot higher than our neighbor's farm because we have adopted the Farming God's Way method of agriculture. Even our rice is of better quality because we do not use artificial fertilizers and chemicals, and the agricultural board in this region has noticed. Because of the successful results, the government has given our farm an award and has also offered us free electricity to pump water over our land. So, we have saved a lot of money on our electricity bill and have used that money to build a large cowshed, without any support from abroad. A tractor was also purchased from the same budget. You can imagine that this was a boost to the self-esteem of our Indian farmers who live under the warm blanket of God's rich blessings.

Some of our adoptive parents wanted to do something other than farming. They asked us if they could start a brick factory. We thought it was a good idea, and so we started a small factory to make cement blocks. This company soon became self-sufficient, and they were able to buy their own machines without a loan. In addition, we now buy the bricks for our multifunctional village churches from our own Abba Cement Block factory—a wonderful win-win situation because they get good business, and we get cheap bricks.

We have started schools in our multifunctional houses where all children from the village are welcome. There, they learn to read, write, and do arithmetic. But most of all, we teach them about Jesus, their Savior. All children, regardless of gender, religion, or tribal background, are welcome to develop their skills. The older children are taught how to use the computer, the women are taught sewing, and the men are taught effective farming methods and/or vocational training.

And all this happens in an atmosphere of God's grace and blessing.

We are seeing community transformation on a micro level. Just a few years ago, these people were despised and looked down upon. Now they have a smile on their face, and they are happy. It is worth turning to the living God. Hallelujah.

Another amazing wonder we saw was related to drought. The weather extremes of both rain and drought are a big problem in India. If it is too wet, the crops rot in the fields. If it is too dry, nothing grows. We learned this lesson the hard way, but our God came to our aid.

In 2019, we completed our fiftieth multifunctional village church. Our dream had become reality. However, that same year, the summer was extremely hot and dry. Kingsly told me on the phone that he expected the harvest to fail that year if rain did not fall soon or if we did not find another way to get water.

While we were praying, we decided to do two things.

First, we decided to purchase the economic drip irrigation system. That is a clever Israeli invention designed to feed the vegetation with just enough water to grow—a small drop of water on the root to save tons of water. No overflow, no loss of precious water. Although we wouldn't benefit much from it that year because everything was already so dry, it would certainly help us in the coming years if there were to be another major drought.

> # WE DID WHAT WE COULD DO, AND THEN GOD DID WHAT WE COULD NOT DO.

Secondly, we decided to dig our wells deeper to gain access to more water. We even decided to dig a new well on the Goshen farm. It was a costly investment, but the loss of the crop could be even more devastating. I raised the money, and Kingsly dug the new well and older wells deeper, hoping to find more water. It was quite difficult because we were not sure that our investment would yield water. So, we prayed and dug. We did what we could do, and then God did what we could not do. He performed an amazing miracle on one of our new farmlands.

THE SOURCE THAT KEPT FLOWING

As the men dug the well deeper, the water level in the well suddenly began to rise, and it kept rising and rising and rising. It even started to overflow the storm wall of the well. It seemed like we had tapped a secret source. Even more amazing is that the other nearby wells were still dry, but ours was overflowing, above and beyond our wildest expectations. Then, God reminded me of 2 Kings 3:16-20 (KJV):

> *Thus saith the LORD, Make this valley full of ditches. For thus saith the LORD, Ye shall not see wind, neither shall ye see rain; yet that valley shall be filled with water, that ye may drink, both ye, and your cattle, and your beasts.*

*And this is but a light thing in the sight of the LORD: he
will deliver the Moabites also into your hand.*

*And ye shall smite every fenced city, and every choice city,
and shall fell every good tree, and stop all wells of water,
and mar every good piece of land with stones.*

How timely and relevant. We had done what we could do,
and God did what we could not do. We dug deeper; we saw
no rain or wind, but the ditches were filled with water. Hallelujah! We could not have imagined that our God would perform
such a miracle of biblical proportions. We saw it as a sign from
heaven, just as this verse said, "And this is but a light thing in the
sight of the LORD."

To God, it was a simple thing, but to us, it was an amazing
miracle. Not only had we been given natural water in a supernatural way to water our fields in the future, but also the promise of
"spiritual water" with which we can harvest souls later. It was not
only an amazing miracle in the natural but also the additional
promise that he would give us the cities and the people whom we
would win for Christ. Hallelujah!

We were all very excited, and our faith was taken to another
level in anticipation of things to come and the harvest of precious
souls we could bring in.

Little did we know, however, that a serious test and trial would
come our way first.

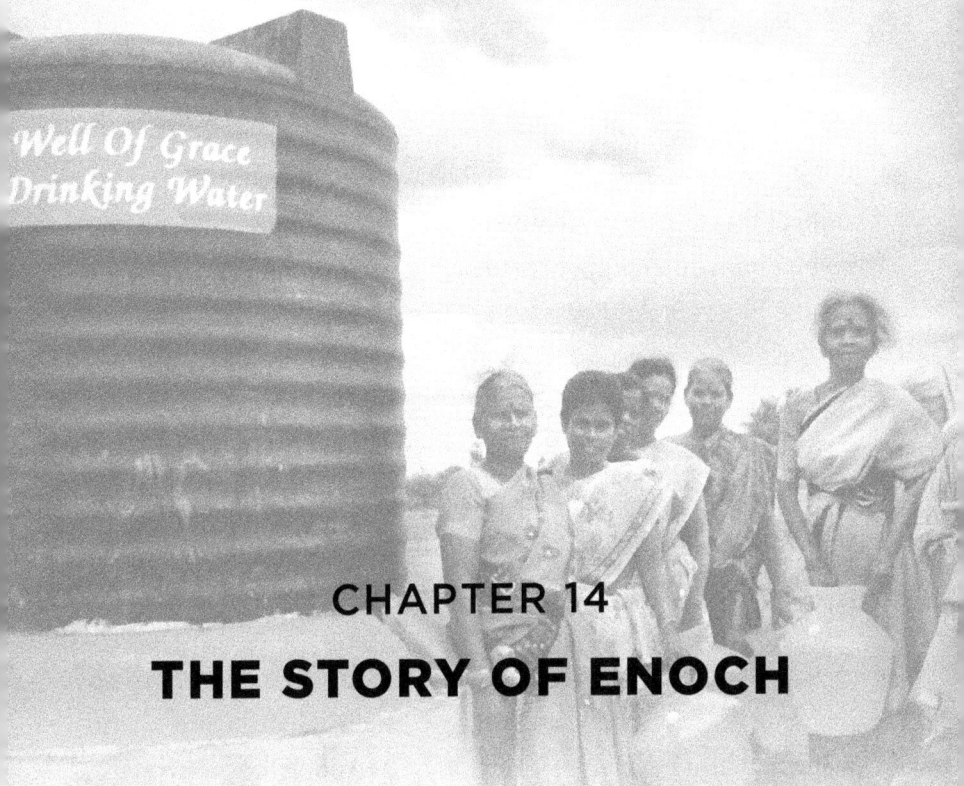

On the photo: *Well Of Grace Drinking Water*

CHAPTER 14

THE STORY OF ENOCH

Meanwhile, Kingsly was still visiting our former friends and colleagues in Andhra Pradesh, Orissa, and Rajasthan from time to time. On one occasion, he visited our friend Enoch in Orissa. Kingsly occasionally supported Enoch in preaching the gospel.

However, this story would take a tragic turn, which made us realize that not everything we did would always be easy and comforting, as the story of Enoch shows. A few weeks after he visited Enoch, Kingsly received a phone call from an unknown man:

"Are you the Kingsly Lazarus?"

"Yes, that's me!"

"Do you know a certain man in Orissa named Enoch?"

"Yes, I do!"

"Will you help him and sponsor him?"

"Yes, why do you ask, and who are you?"

"It doesn't matter who I am, but we are communists, and we control this territory. We want you to know that we will kill you if you ever dare to come here to help Enoch again. We don't want people like you. And besides, we have captured your friend and twelve of his disciples, and you will never see them alive again!"

Click. End of phone call.

Kingsly was stunned. However, he had an application on his phone that recorded every conversation. He suddenly realized that Enoch and his friends were in grave danger. He had to act quickly to see if he could find help to save Enoch and his twelve friends.

Because of the large children's home in Orissa, Kingsly had developed a good relationship with the local authorities, who respected him immensely for what he had done for the orphans, some of whose parents had been murdered during the bloody Christian persecution in 2008. He immediately called the local police station and asked for the chief of police. He told him that his friends were in mortal danger and that immediate action was required. He gave him the phone number of the communist rebel captain to trace his location and asked him to send a rescue team immediately to save Enoch and his men. The police chief politely replied, "Yes sir, yes sir!"

Kingsly knew the culture and realized that sometimes the authorities say yes but still do nothing. So just to be safe, he responded and said, "Listen to me! Our conversation is being recorded on my phone. If you just say yes but do nothing, my friends could die. Then, I will send this recorded message to the governor, whom I know personally. It will prove that you lied to me at the cost of the lives of my friends. Do you hear what I am saying? So, take immediate action to save these precious lives!"

The police commissioner realized his great responsibility and vowed to take immediate action. And thank God he did. They traced the location of the rebel leader's phone, sent a rescue team, and surprised the rebels. Fortunately, they arrived just in time to save Enoch and his men. The rebel captain must have realized that Kingsly was a very influential man, that he was able to track them down quickly and at the same time mobilize a rescue team to free his friends.

But Enoch and his twelve friends were all sorely smitten on the soles of their feet that none of them could walk. So, the authorities brought them to the hospital to treat their wounds. We were so grateful that none of them were killed. Enoch was not only struck on his feet. As the leader of this group, he was severely beaten on his chest and back, causing deep internal wounds to his liver and kidneys. Unfortunately, that was not visible on the outside. So, they brought him home, but he was too weak to function and was confined to bed due to these internal injuries. Slowly but surely, Enoch became sicker and sicker.

Kingsly called Enoch to ask about his well-being, and he prayed on the phone. But as Enoch was getting worse day by day, Kingsly decided to pay him a visit. He traveled by car with his right-hand man, Babu, and his father-in-law, Patrick, to Orissa to visit Enoch and pray for him.

Just as they began to pray for Enoch, the house was suddenly surrounded by a biker gang. They pressed a gun to Kingsly's head and forced him, Babu, and Patrick into the car immediately. At gunpoint, he was forced to follow the motorcycles. They ended up in a forest area and went deeper and deeper into the jungle. Finally, they stopped in a small field in the middle of the jungle. There, they were ordered to sit down on the ground and wait.

- They had no idea who these guys were.
- They had no idea why they had been captured.
- They had no idea why they were being targeted.
- They had no idea what would happen to them.
- They had no idea what to expect.
- They had no idea how this would end.

Kingsly thought, "This might as well be my last hour. Maybe we'll be killed and go to heaven. Is this the last day of my life on earth? Will I see Jesus and my grandfather soon? What about my dear Anita and my boys? O God, I place my life in Your hands," he prayed.

After waiting for what seemed like hours, a car arrived with the rebel captain.

"So here you are, Mr. Kingsly. I told you not to come here anymore, but you ignored my warning. However, I will give you a chance to escape if you do as I say!"

Throwing a piece of paper to Kingsly, he said, "I want a hundred thousand dollars and two of my men back from prison in exchange for your freedom."

Kingsly looked at the paper and realized that it was the financial statements on the Abba Child Care website. In the Netherlands, it is mandatory to include the annual financial reports on the site, but this information was on a (more or less) hidden page. Yet these guys had traced our information and knew the amounts that had been transferred to Sharing Hands. They demanded this huge sum of money as a sort of fine for violating their restraining order, along with the release of two of their men who were in prison in exchange for Kingsly's, Babu's, and Patrick's release.

Kingsly said, "Sir, we don't have this money. All this money is invested in saving children, feeding the poor, caring for widows, providing medical care, and building wells. If we had the money, I would give it to you, but we don't have that amount. I'm sorry! If we try our best, we may be able to give you twenty thousand dollars."

They prayed for God to intervene, and God answered their cry, for the captain accepted Kingsly's proposal. He gave him a telephone and said, "Call anyone you like to arrange for the money and the release of our men." Kingsly called the governor of Orissa and explained the situation. Thank God for the good relationship Kingsly had developed with the governor over the years. And thank God, the governor took immediate action to arrange for the ransom of $20,000 and the rescue of two of their men from prison. It took several hours for the money and men to be delivered in exchange for Kingsly, Babu, and Patrick.

Three precious and priceless human lives and a nice van for a sum of only $20,000. That is really cheap! We are so thankful to God that they are still alive. It could have ended so tragically.

Fortunately, they were more interested in our money than our lives. Money is replaceable, but life is not. This adventure fizzled out. We also prayed that this would not become another way for the rebels to get money.

Tragically, our dear friend Enoch died of his wounds a short time later. It was an indirect assassination by these rebels. Kingsley was very sad and said to Enoch's wife that he wanted to travel to Orissa again to show sympathy and comfort her. He informed me of this, but I strongly warned him not to go because if the rebels found him again, they might kill him. I said to Kingsly: "Dear Kingsly, please don't go! At least not unless the governor can guarantee your safety."

Unfortunately, the governor could not guarantee the safety of Kingsly. The jungle in that area was completely under the control of the communist rebel groups. Because we felt so sorry for the widow of Enoch, his children, and the fellow Christians who now lost their leader, we felt we had to do something. We decided to support Enoch's widow, but we also wanted to create a memorial. So, we decided to dig a well in memory of our friend, Enoch. We called him "source of grace."

We know and believe that Enoch did not die in vain. From his home, the fountain of grace would continue to flow through this country, which is still controlled by the rebels to this day. For the blood of the martyrs is the seed of the church!

Fortunately, our ventures birthed more than just tragic stories. In fact, most of the stories are very encouraging and inspiring. One such story is the story of Babu.

CHAPTER 15

THE STORY OF BABU

For years and years, Babu has been Kingsly's inseparable right hand. But in this story, we will see how that came about. Baby Babu was abandoned in a church by his penniless mother. She was too poor to take care of him, so she hoped that the people in the church would. It was not easy for little Babu. He often cried because he missed his mother. Fortunately, he was lovingly taken in by the Lazarus family as one of the first children under their care. Kingsly was just a little boy when Babu came to the family. At first, Kingsly didn't know any better—to him, Babu was his big brother as they grew up together in a loving family. Indeed, since then, they have been together as brothers. In the Lazarus household, Babu heard about God and Jesus every day. He loved the Bible stories and couldn't get enough of them. So, the Word of God was planted in his young heart, and slowly, his heart was healed from the pain of missing his mother. Babu was an active and energetic boy. He got good grades in school. At home, he helped with all kinds of practical jobs in and around the house. In the meantime, he learned God's grace and was getting to know the Word better and better.

As he grew older, he developed a desire to tell the people in his home village about Jesus. Knowing that Jesus alone is the true God, he wanted his fellow villagers to know the living God and be freed from idolatry. The burden on his heart for the lost souls in his village, who were blind and bound by all sorts of Hindu rituals and traditions, grew ever greater. Almost all of the people in his village were Dalits, and because the Dalits were not allowed to enter the temple, they did not have a temple in their village. However, they had a "holy stone" in their village, which they regarded as their temple and which became their place of worship. In times of need, the poor Dalits turned in their ignorance to this stone to offer sacrifices, hoping to get an answer to their prayers.

Babu knew better now, and he wanted his fellow villagers to know the true Savior, who really answers prayers, just as he had seen so many times since he had been with the Lazarus family.

A WHOLE VILLAGE BAPTIZED

Babu prayed to God and even fasted in his desire to reach the people of his native place. After his studies, he returned to his village, where the people still made offerings at the "holy stone" to appease their gods. Even his own mother was caught in these senseless rituals.

His heart went out to them, and he began to share God's love as much as he could. At first, he had no success. It felt like a waste of time. But Babu did not give up. Slowly but surely, his witness began to penetrate their hearts, and they began to listen to his passionate pleas. One by one, they responded to the gospel and believed in Jesus.

It seemed as if God Himself was manifesting His love as more and more people gave their lives to Jesus. The news spread like wildfire through the region. More and more people wanted to hear about Jesus. Eventually, the whole village turned to Christ and wanted to be baptized. What to do now? Babu did not know. So, he sought the help of a missionary. All in one day, an entire village—from the oldest to the youngest—was baptized.

People from the surrounding villages joined this joyful celebration. A buffalo was slaughtered, and a meal was cooked for everyone.

The "holy stone" disappeared. Over time, the desire arose to have their own meeting place where they could worship God. They prayed for it every day until someone suggested the idea of using the land on which their "holy stone" once stood. After all, they no longer believed in those idols! They decided to smash the stone and build a house for God on the same spot.

Together, they prayed for the miracle of a church because they did not have the money or the skills to build one. It was not long before their fervent prayers were answered.

When we started building churches and saw the dedication and love of these villagers, we decided to build a church in Babu's village, too.

So, the idol stone was destroyed, and a house of God was built on the same spot. The foundation stone was laid, and this festive day has been celebrated every year since then, beginning with a week of fasting and ending with a meal to celebrate their deliverance from idols. The joy of the people was overwhelming.

A SOURCE OF BLESSING

All this happened because of the persistent efforts of a young man. Despite his dramatic start in life, his love and passion for God and people made him a source of blessing to his entire village.

When Babu grew up, he found his beloved Selvi. He married her, and they had a beautiful daughter and adopted an orphan boy—remarkable since Babu himself was once an orphan. Who knows how his adopted son would bless others in the future as he did.

Moreover, Babu is the right hand of our partner, Kingsly Lazarus, in all our projects in India. He is an example to many because of his passion and zeal for God. They have experienced many things together, as you have read in the story of his friend, Enoch. Their love for each other is like the friendship of Jonathan and David. Jonathan was so devoted to David that he even risked the wrath of his own father. I saw that level of commitment in Babu's heart, as the following story demonstrates.

One day, the leader of a very large and well-known ministry in India, who has been associated with the Lazarus family for many years, visited Kingsly. This man noticed Babu's solid character, his dedication, and his servant's heart, so he wanted Babu to join him in his work in the United States. He asked Kingsly if he could recommend Babu for this promising position. If he said yes, he would travel to America and be given a house, a car, a good salary, and much more. This would have been a very attractive proposition for Babu, a man living a simple life in a small house while working day and night to support Kingsly in all his responsibilities.

What a tempting opportunity for a small village boy. But not for Babu. His answer to this proposal was simple and clear: "Only death can part me from Kingsly!"

I was deeply moved when I heard this and was proud to be associated with such good, faithful, yet humble men of God. He is one of the great reasons for the success of this ministry.

There are many precious lessons to be learned, especially through these often simple men, who understand the heartbeat of God and are faithful to the core.

CHAPTER 16

A MODERN CINDERELLA STORY

On a cold evening, Patrick brought his wife, Selvi, to the clinic because her contractions had started. When the clock struck midnight on October 16, 1980, he heard the first cries of his newborn baby. It was a girl, and they called her Anita. Anita's story seems like an old fairy tale; however, this story is a real, modern Cinderella story.

It was raining cats and dogs when Patrick and Selvi left the clinic early in the morning. Their poor, shabby thatched hut had been almost flooded, and the roof leaked in many places. Patrick found a piece of plastic along the road that he threw over the roof to stop it from leaking so much.

With great effort and pain in his heart, he tried to create a dry and safe place for their beautiful little girl. As it continued to rain for days, they were very concerned about how this cold and foggy weather would affect the health of the little girl.

Patrick was a man of prayer and a faithful follower of Jesus. Both he and Selvi were active members in their church. You can imagine how they prayed for God's intervention in this dire circumstance. They had no idea how God would soon answer their prayers. As the rain continued to fall, they were constantly struggling to stay dry in their small hut. In order to keep little Anita dry, Patrick had made a kind of basket out of a sari and hung it on one of the beams of their hut, away from the wet and muddy floor. While Patrick went to work and little Anita was fast asleep, Selvi quickly rushed to the market to buy some food. With no one to care for the baby, she had no other choice.

FROM THE WELL TO THE PALACE

Meanwhile, Srinivasan and his wife Nirmala were passing by their hut and heard a baby crying. Curious and moved by Anita's cries, they could not resist looking inside the poor hut, where they found little Anita. Moved with pity and worried that the child might catch a cold, Mrs. Nirmala took the baby out of her basket and pressed it to her heart. She was struck with strong emotions when little Anita smiled at her.

Nirmala looked at her husband. When their eyes met, it was clear that both felt they had to do something to help this poor family in need. They stood silently pondering.

Still weak and tired from childbirth, Selvi rushed back to her hut. When she entered, she was shocked to see her little baby in the arms of a rich lady. They were obviously high caste people, and Selvi was clearly a Dalit, or rather a casteless untouchable.

Many high caste people do not even want the shadow of a Dalit to fall on them, but this high-ranking lady was gently and lovingly kissing this little Dalit girl in her arms. Selvi was afraid of what would happen next, but Mrs. Nirmala put Selvi at ease. She apologized kindly and assured Selvi that she and her husband had only good intentions. They told Selvi that they wanted to help her and her baby. Nirmala immediately fell in love with little Anita and assured Selvi that she wanted to take care of her and adopt her.

THE HIGHEST OF THE HIGH EMBRACED THE LOWEST OF THE LOW.

"Don't get me wrong—when I say I want to adopt her, we also want to adopt you and your husband along with her. Why don't you come with us and live in our home where we can provide good care for you, your husband, and your baby?"

That day, the highest of the high embraced the lowest of the low.

Was she dreaming? Had she really heard those words? She didn't know what to think or say. It was too good to be true. But what if it really was true? Selvi's mind was spinning, and she obviously couldn't decide without her husband's approval.

"Well, I have to talk to my husband about that first, who is now working!"

Stunned and anxious, she waited the rest of the day for Patrick to come home. With tears in her eyes, she told him what had happened. They soon discovered that this was real and joyfully accepted Srinivasan and Nirmala's gracious offer. That night, for the first time, they slept in a real house. The house of an upper caste family—the highest caste, because Mr. Srinivasan was a Brahmin. It would take some time for Patrick and Selvi to process the full impact of the miracle, and that was just the beginning of this amazing story.

Mr. Srinivasan assured them that they would give Anita a very good life and that they wanted to adopt her as their own child, but that Patrick and Selvi would remain her legal parents. And that's what they did because they loved Anita as much as they loved their own daughter, Viji. Together, they grew up as sisters, and Patrick and Selvi lived with them as a forever family.

Anita's adoptive mother, Nirmala, was a famous film singer. She was also a devout Christian and not ashamed to sing about Jesus. Anita enjoyed Nirmala's singing and wanted to sing herself, so Nirmala often took her along to her concerts, where little Anita sang along with her adoptive mother. Moreover, Anita received the best education in the best schools of Chennai. They wanted to give Anita a good life and a hopeful future. It was as if Selvi was dreaming, but this was not a dream. It really happened! Yet it took a while before Selvi could accept the blessed reality. She was overwhelmed, happy, and shocked at the same time.

Anita was only five days old when she moved with her mom and dad to Srinivasan and Nirmala's beautiful villa. They couldn't believe their eyes when they entered this beautiful home. In just one day, God had turned their situation completely upside down!

What a privilege that their sweet little Anita was able to grow up in such a beautiful place!

Despite the religious prejudice against Dalits, Nirmala Srinivasan did not hesitate to take them in and love them as their own flesh and blood.

Revolutionary!

Patrick and Selvi were incredibly grateful for the new life they had found with the Srinivasan family. Nirmala also found Patrick a good job at the Highway Department. He was so grateful for this extra blessing.

Nirmala was a famous singer, and Anita also loved to sing. Because of Nirmala's fame, Anita got many opportunities to sing with her in her concerts. She was not afraid but sang courageously in front of thousands of people about God's love. She had no idea that one day, God would use her love for music in such a great way. Anita grew up loving and respecting her parents, adoptive parents, and her sister Viji. Anita received her bachelor's degree from the College in Chennai.

She became a great singer and a beautiful young woman.

Sadly, in 2000, Nirmala became seriously ill and died. This was not only a great blow to Srinivasan but also to Anita, as she had learned so much and received so much love from Nirmala. In the meantime, Anita obtained a degree in human resource development and psychology from the University of Madras. Grateful and very aware of the extraordinary turn in her life, she decided to dedicate her life to God and bring hope and help to baby girls like herself.

A MATCH MADE IN HEAVEN

In keeping with Indian tradition, Anita's parents and adoptive father searched for a potential life partner for Anita. Arranged marriages are still customary in Indian culture. As devout Christians, they were looking for a young man devoted to loving God. They found that lucky man in none other than Kingsly, the son of Pastor John and Rachel Lazarus.

Finally, on June 9, 2004, Kingsly and Anita got married. At the wedding, Anita was given to Kingsly by both her own father, Patrick, and her adoptive father, Srinivasan. No one knew what great plans God had for this young couple.

As time unfolded, their union proved to be the perfect match—a "match made in heaven"—as they say in English. They have been happily married for years now and are blessed with three children: Richard, Reynold, and Anna. The story is like a modern version of Cinderella, only this is not a fairy tale, but a dream come true.

TWO "HOPELESS" CHILDREN

This is the story of Anita, a poverty-stricken and hopeless Dalit baby, who was taken from her poor hut and into a wealthy villa five days after her birth.

And it is the story of Kingsly, who often went to bed hungry because his parents were so poor that they could barely afford food. During the day, he would collect leftovers from the open sewer near his school to fill his hungry stomach.

Two hopelessly poor and underprivileged children with little or no hope for a bright future were chosen by God to have a hopeful future. They now help thousands of poor and disadvantaged people and children by providing them with a hopeful future.

And I, Jaap Dieleman, once a street vagrant and drug addict, have had the unique privilege of becoming their true friend and partner in this great work. What a great and wonderful God we serve. Indeed, it is so true what God's Word says: "What no eye has seen, nor ear heard, nor the heart of man imagined, what God has prepared for those who love him" (1 Corinthians 2:9, ESV).

And I haven't even told half of the story yet—this is just the beginning of Abba Child Care's history. Little did we know that God would take us on an even greater adventure.

CHAPTER 17

MIRACLES IN CHENGALPATTU

Every time we drove to the Uthiramerur district, where we started our first farm and built our first multi-purpose church building, we made a stop for coffee on the highway south, before turning right to Uthiramerur.

I was curious about what was on the other side of the road every time we stopped there. I asked Kingsly:

"Who lives there? Who among them has heard the gospel? Shouldn't we share the gospel there, too? What is the most important city there?"

Kingsly replied, "Chengalpattu, Pastor. Chengalpattu is the most important town there!"

COME OVER AND HELP US

"The other side" kept coming to me every time we stopped for that cup of coffee. On one of these occasions, I was reminded of Paul's dream of this Macedonian man who called Paul to come to him and help him. Paul got the impression that this was God's way of speaking to him, and so he looked for ways to go to Macedonia. I felt inspired by the Holy Spirit to share my thoughts about the other side of the road with Kingsly. However, Kingsly had no contacts in that region, and he was not very excited about going there, either, since that area was known to be very hostile toward the gospel. Furthermore, he had no idea what to do with my impression of the other side. But then, God started to set things in motion.

Several Christian churches had heard what God was doing in Uthiramerur from Mr. Murthy, the mayor of Marudham. They heard about the churches, the miracles, the Bible school we had started, the farm, and everything else God was doing. Their hunger and thirst were triggered as they heard Mr. Murthy tell the wonderful stories.

So, they decided to visit Kingsly and ask him to "come and help them." Wow! Kingsly received his Macedonian call from Chengalpattu itself. It seemed that God had waited until the right moment to confirm this in Kingsly's spirit. So, we made our first visit to "the other side."

When we got there, we decided to build wells and multipurpose churches. So, our region was extended to Chengalpattu, and it is not surprising that our area would slowly but surely extend beyond Chengalpattu to the Cheyyur region.

Later, we would buy even more beautiful farmland for our adoptive families in the Cheyyur region. Little did we know that this would only be a stepping stone to an even bigger plan that would reach the entire state of Tamilnadu!

But first, let us see how God worked in amazing ways in Chengalpattu.

Over the years that followed, we dug fifty wells there, and because there were so few churches, we felt called to build more in Chengalpattu as we did in Uthiramerur. Through our growing contacts and friendships in this region, we felt tempted to also build a gospel church in the city of Chengalpattu and hold a festival on the grounds of a large bus station.

When I arrived to India with my team, the entrance to the festival was like a gate and at the end of the field was the stage. Anyone who walked past the gate could immediately see that something festive was going on with music, singing, and dancing. Slowly but surely, the square filled up, and thousands of people came to it.

I was asked not to preach to avoid problems with the authorities. So, just like the Living Water Festival, I instead told the story of drilling the wells and drinking the Living Water. Hidden in parables, I shared the core message of the gospel, more or less. In doing so, I emphasized drinking the Living Water, which would quench their thirst forever. Kingsly was my translator so that the people could understand the message in their local language.

In the middle of my speech, I suddenly said, "Why should you drink that bottle of poison and die? You are not here by chance. Please come to Jesus and drink of the water of life that Jesus gives, and you will live life in abundance!"

Kingsly looked at me a little worried about what I was saying, but I insisted that he translate it. Even I did not know why I said it, but I concluded: "And if you want to drink that Living Water, please listen to the preacher; he will tell you how to get it!" Then I turned to Kingsly and told him to make the invitation as a preacher. I disappeared from the platform to avoid awkward questions from civilian officers and the police, while Kingsly continued to call people to receive Christ and come and drink the Living Water. It was only after the meeting that we heard the amazing testimony of one man who came forward to receive Christ. He said:

> I had just bought a bottle of poison in the market because I wanted to end my miserable life. As I passed the bus station, I heard the white man talking about drinking the Living Water. And then he said, "Why would you drink that bottle of poison and die?" as if he knew that I had a bottle of poison in my hand. And then he continued, "Please come forward to Jesus and drink the Living Water! At that moment, the bottle of poison fell from my hand to the ground and broke. When the pastor then invited us to come forward, I felt the pull of God's love and ran forward to drink from the Living Water of life!

We were all amazed at how God had spoken through me at the right time to this desperate man who was about to commit suicide. Besides this great testimony, we counted more than 3,000 decisions for Jesus that night, and on top of that, God did many other miracles of healing and deliverance in Chengalpattu.

What a joy it is to serve our God, and let's face it: He is in charge, He is leading us, He is guiding us, He is directing our steps. We are just witnesses to all the great things He is doing. Even more amazing is realizing that He wants to use simple people like us to make His love and His power known to others.

BLESSING FESTIVAL IN KOOVATHUR

Besides our projects in agriculture, medical care, widows, orphans, lepers, education, and others, our main focus and heartbeat is sharing the love of God through Christ. In fact, all our projects are based on the heartbeat of this fundamental command. Sometimes, however, the Lord leads in very peculiar ways—ways that are least expected!

Although I am not afraid of a challenge, I think Kingsly takes the cake. Kingsly likes to take on the challenge of crawling into the "lion's den," so to speak. One time, Kingsly felt led to organize a festival in the village of Koovathur. The previous year, Sasi, one of our dear brothers, was cruelly tortured and murdered in Koovathur. That alone should have been reason enough not to go to Koovathur. Kingsly, however, thought it was right to organize a gospel festival there. This would be God's "counterattack," striking back with love. A number of team members who had come with me anxiously wondered if it was a good idea. But we said to the team, "Listen, Sasi's life was sown as a very precious seed in the Indian soil, and now, in this new harvest season, we are going back to reap a great harvest of precious souls for Christ. We know that our dear brother did not die in vain, because we will see the fruit of his labor."

> ## "WE HAVE TO BUILD A CHURCH HERE," AND GOD WHISPERED IN SOMEONE ELSE'S EAR, "YOU MUST SPONSOR A CHURCH!"

These words encouraged and strengthened us all. So, we prayed and obeyed the call of God. The atmosphere was very joyful and peaceful, despite the recent attack. I brought some musicians. Mattanja played the violin and Ronald the keyboard, singing in Western style. The audience, who were used to the typical Indian style of worship, were joyfully attracted to and surprised by the style of this Western worship music. It prepared their hearts to receive the message of God's love. Ultimately, we saw over a thousand people saved during this crusade, and many miracles of healing and deliverance took place. This was very reassuring and a great encouragement to the local Christian community, which had been so badly affected the previous year.

I whispered in Kingsly's ear: "We have to build a church here," and God whispered in someone else's ear, "You must sponsor a church!"

A NEW CHURCH FOR KOOVATHUR

Although we wanted to strengthen the fifty multifunctional churches that we had built up to that point, I felt that we should build church number fifty-one in Koovathur first. I felt that God wanted to bless and encourage the local Christian community with their own place of worship. Furthermore, I believed it was also necessary to consolidate the great harvest of precious souls that was gathered during the Blessing Festival.

At the same time that I heard God ask me to build a church in Koovathur, I received a phone call from this brother who was greatly encouraged when he heard my side of the story. He immediately transferred the money, and the construction was started.

Talk about guidance from the Holy Spirit! You often only see His guidance in retrospect. When I had whispered those words in Kingsly's ear, I had no idea that God had whispered in this brothers ear to sponsor a church, not knowing that he was an answer to our prayer. God had started moving before I had even prayed about it.

As I said, we often see His mighty hand in hindsight, and that was the case with the new land we wanted to buy, which was far beyond our means.

But God opened the windows of heaven and made the impossible possible.

CHAPTER 18

GOD OPENED THE WINDOWS OF HEAVEN

As our agricultural project began to take off, more children were brought to us for adoption. On an annual basis, we see an average of one hundred new orphans brought to us for adoption. In order to place these children in an adoptive family and provide this family with a piece of land, we needed more land. So, we went looking for more agricultural land to buy. Fertile agricultural land in India is quite expensive, so it was a big challenge. We prayed that God would open the windows of heaven, and amazingly, he did so in the Cheyyur district.

Mr. Chettiar, a wealthy farmer from Cheyyur, had a son who was going to study in America. In order to pay for his studies, he decided to sell some of his farmland. Generally, wealthy Hindu farmers do not want to sell land to Christians because of religious differences, and they certainly do not want to sell it if it is used to sponsor Dalits and orphans. But Mr. Chettiar was different—at least, that is what we discovered when we started negotiating the purchase of his farmland.

It so happened that one of our Dalit adoptive parents who lived in the Cheyyur area worked for this man. His job was to iron his clothes. Every now and then, he would chat with Mr. Chettiar. For example, on time, this man told Mr. Cheyyur that he and his wife had adopted an orphan girl through the Abba Family Homes project. This man spoke fondly about his adopted daughter and told Mr. Chettiar that Abba Child Care also provided them with an income from the Abba farm. "Now they are looking for more land so they can help more orphans!" he told his boss. Mr. Chettiar was deeply moved by what he heard. He reasoned to himself:

> *I am so rich but do nothing to help these poor people. But my bonded laborer, who irons my clothes for a few rupees, even takes care of an abandoned baby girl with his meager income. And this organization is even willing to buy land to help more poor Dalit families and street children. What moves these people? What passion drives them? It is certainly a good thing to help them by selling my farmland to them.*

Mr. Chettiar was willing to sell his land to us because it was for a good cause. We made an appointment to visit the two pieces of land he wanted to sell. One was a flat field, good for rice and other vegetation. The second piece was mainly a mango farm that produces twenty-eight tons of mangoes per year. Both farms were very fertile, peaceful and very beautiful. We fell in love immediately and felt that this was the right land to buy. In total, it was almost fourteen hectares of land—enough to house another 660 families who would adopt an orphan. Wow!

We were so happy, but he wanted €750,000 for the land. That was an astonishingly large amount that we did not have. We only had €100,000 in our pot. Despite our lack of money, we felt that this was the land we had to buy. We told the owner to give us some time to raise the money.

We began to pray fervently for a miracle of God's provision, and as we had seen earlier, our Heavenly Father opened the windows of heaven and poured out His blessing upon us.

THE WINDOWS OF HEAVEN WERE OPENED

Shortly after, I visited one of our loyal sponsors and shared the vision of this land and how it would provide space for another 660 Dalit families and orphans. As I shared, I saw tears welling up in the man's eyes. I felt a strong urge to pray for him. "Shall I pray for you?" I asked. The man nodded with a lump in his throat and tears in his eyes. What had happened? Both of us sat there with tears in our eyes, not even knowing why we were so touched by God's presence. After prayer, the man looked at me with tears in his eyes and then said, "Please go and buy that land. I will give you €500,000." I nearly fell off his chair, not knowing what to say.

"Shall I call Kingsly and give him the good news?"

"Yes, go ahead!" he said.

When Kingsly heard the news, he started crying on the other end of the line. It was like we were dreaming, but it was real. God had touched the heart of this passionate man to stand with us and make the impossible possible.

With our own resources and this donation, we already had €600,000. But we were still short €150,000. The fear of being unable to raise the remaining amount came over me with force, but I resisted this fearful thought and strengthened myself in the Lord. Over the years, I had learned that God is faithful. He would not just give us 80 percent and then abandon us for the rest. I recognized the voice of the enemy trying to intimidate me and declared:

"Devil, you are a liar! God will not give us 80 percent first and then abandon us. He will surely complete what He has started, and I declare in the name of Jesus that there will be full provision, and we shall be up to the task until it is complete!"

I felt God lift me above that fear and left everything in the hands of the Lord. Fortunately, it was not long before another sponsor donated the remaining €150,000. Hallelujah! Now we could close the deal.

A MISTAKE IN OUR FAVOR

The land had to be measured and registered before it could be officially transferred. But when the people from the land registry came to measure, they discovered that they had forgotten to include a strip of land on the east side. It represented a value of no less than €75,000. Mr. Chettiar apologized for the mistake and told us that we had to pay an additional amount of €75,000. "We are sorry sir, but we cannot afford to pay more money!" we said. Mr. Chettiar remained silent for a moment, looking at the ground. Then he raised his head, looked Kingsly straight in the eye, and said, "I am so sorry for my mistake; that is why I am giving you this extra 1.5 hectares for free!"

Imagine . . . we had never had a donation of that size from an Indian, and what's even more amazing is that it was from a Hindu man.

Kingsly was overcome with tears of joy when he called me to tell me the wonderful news. All along, God had been there for our needs and had provided again in such a special way.

There was, however, one more obstacle we had to clear. When the landowner wanted to transfer the land for the agreed price, the government became suspicious. They thought that we were making a black mark on this difference. No matter what Mr. Chettiar said, they would not believe him and demanded an investigation. They even investigated our accounts to see if we had somehow made this amount disappear from our account. They could not find any error in their search, neither in Mr. Chettiar's account nor in our accounts. Finally, they accepted the papers, and we were able to transfer the land to our account.

During my next visit to India, I insisted on seeing the land myself and meeting the landowner. The landowner also wanted to meet me because he was so inspired by Abba Child Care's mission and got behind our benevolent and selfless work. I thought about what I would like to give this man. Money, property, wealth—he had more than enough of it. But what was he missing? Suddenly, I knew what I had to give him—a Bible. I would explain how this book was our inspiration for starting all these projects. God's book was the source of our wealth, wisdom, and light in our lives.

> # FOR IN THIS BOOK IS LIFE, IN THIS BOOK IS LOVE, AND IN THIS BOOK IS LIGHT.

So, I asked Kingsly to buy a nice Bible in their language and to include some worship CDs that his father had produced.

At the meeting, I thanked Mr. Chettiar very much for his wonderful donation, which was one-tenth of the original amount. Moreover, he was the first Hindu man who had been so generous to us. I told him that God would richly bless him for his investment in God's work. I then handed him the Bible and explained how this book had been our guide, our anchor, and our source of inspiration. I added: "For in this book is life, in this book is love, and in this book is light." He then took the Bible with both hands and pressed it to his heart. For Westerners, this may seem insignificant, but in Asia and India, accepting a gift with both hands is a sign of great appreciation. We had no idea how much this book meant to this man, but we would soon find out.

Before I left, I noticed that Mr. Chettiar had a new car. On the windshield, I read the words "Jesus is Lord", and on the back window was a Bible verse written in Tamil. What had happened to this man? As we were about to leave, his manager came to pick up the keys to the house we had rented. He surprisingly told us:

When we went home, he demonstratively put the Bible on the table with both hands and said to his wife, "I don't know what you are going to do, but I am going to follow

*this book, because the man of God told me, 'In this book is
Light, in this book is Love, and in this Book is Life!'"*
What an amazing testimony from a Hindu man who openly
sponsored God's work and actually paid his first tithe right away.
In his words, he professed to be a follower of Christ and affirmed
his intention to follow God's Word.

HALLELUJAH TO THE LORD!

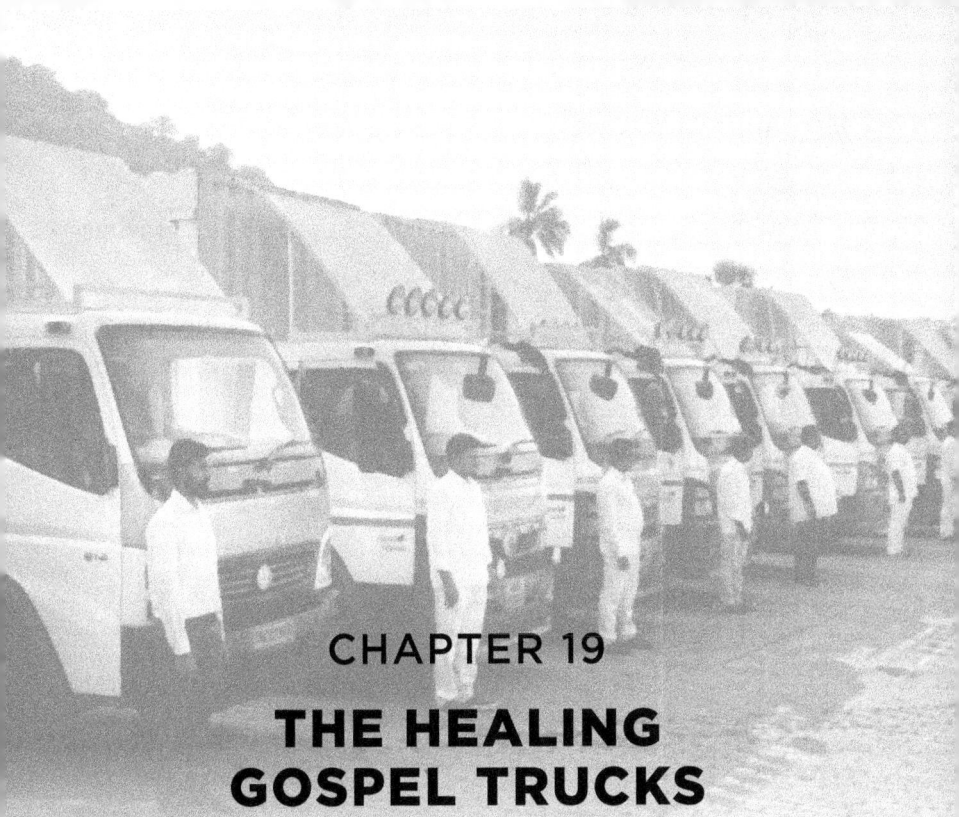

CHAPTER 19

THE HEALING GOSPEL TRUCKS

In the meantime, we wanted to share the gospel, the good news of Jesus Christ, with these poor villagers. So, in addition to our development projects of providing land, drilling water points, distributing food, and helping widows and orphans, we organized regular meetings to share the good news of Jesus with these dear people, but we first had to go to each village and ask permission. When permission was granted, there were always a few willing villagers who wanted to build a stage for us. We also rented a generator, a sound system, and some lighting. Usually, the locals felt honored to provide these things, and it became a small source of income for them. We managed to win the favor of the villagers.

However, most of the time, the stage was so wobbly and unstable that it was scary to stand on, and often, it was too small for a speaker and a translator to stand on together.

In addition, they sometimes connected the electrical wires by tying bare copper wire together. To make matters worse, the quality of the generator and the sound system was sometimes so poor that the crackling sound of the generator made more noise through the microphone than the speaker's voice.

Periodically, the generator would fail, and we would be plunged into total darkness and deathly silence. Nevertheless, we did everything we could to share the good news, and God blessed our efforts. We saw people come to Christ and many healed and delivered. But at the same time, I felt that we needed to find a better, simpler, and easier way to hold these meetings. And so out of these struggles, a new vision was born. A vision for a gospel truck.

THE GOSPEL TRUCK

The idea was to build a truck with a container, equipped with a hydraulic side door, which could be folded down to become a stage. We considered putting batteries under the truck that would charge as we drove, so that when we drove into a small town, we would have enough power for the sound system and lights for several hours while we shared the good news. So, we started researching the size of the car, the prices, and the cost of building one with a sound and light system. We discovered that we could build the truck for about €25,000—a considerable amount, but still very cheap when compared to the price of these trucks in Europe. We prayed that God would move the hearts of sponsors to help us realize this dream, and He did.

So, we first launched the vision in December 2017, and by the end of 2018, our first gospel truck went on the road. We befriended a couple from Belgium who was the first to invest in building our gospel truck. Even though there were still a few imperfections in the first model, the truck made our attempts to reach a village so much easier.

We drove into a village, parked the car in a central spot, and opened the hydraulic side door. The stage was ready for a meeting.

Within half an hour, everything was ready to bring the gospel. After the first visit, the truck was packed again within half an hour to visit the next town. What a great improvement. People in these remote villages rarely saw such a big, colorful truck!

When we entered a village, many children would immediately run to us, and the news about this big gospel truck spread like wildfire. It would not be long before the whole village came curiously to see who we were and what we were doing. We easily attracted a crowd of 300 to 700 villagers to come and watch the event. That was, of course, quite a feat in these normally quiet villages, where almost nothing ever happens. In order to hold the audience until the end, we had prepared bags of rice to give to these mostly very poor people. However, they would only receive their bag of rice after they had heard the message. So we would first have them "eat the bread of life" before they would receive a bag of rice.

Many people stayed and opened their hearts to Jesus because that was our main goal. In addition, we saw great miracles and happy faces when we gave them a bag of rice. With this new tool in our hands, we realized what a blessing the gospel truck was.

> ## WE GAVE THEM THE BREAD OF LIFE BEFORE WE GAVE THEM A BAG OF RICE.

ANOTHER GOSPEL TRUCK

In the meantime, we went to a small village where we held a meeting with our first gospel truck. Kingsly had once again entered the lion's den by positioning our gospel truck right across from a Hindu temple.

Nevertheless, over 300 people responded to the gospel and gave their lives to Jesus. At this first try-out, I noticed a few flaws in the truck. The hydraulic side—which served as a platform—was not high enough and too wobbly. Something had to be done about its stability. Also, the truck needed a lock so that it wouldn't open as we drove it on the highway.

I told Kingsly that we had to improve the next truck. We needed a safety lock for the hydraulic door, stabilizers for the truck so that we could stand on bumpy ground. We needed to make the stage a bit higher so that we could stand on it without hitting our heads on the ceiling. "We must solve these problems for the next truck!" I said. Kingsly smiled. We had never talked about a second truck before.

So, I looked up in surprise and laughed. "Don't you want a second truck?" I asked Kingsly. He responded, "Yes, pastor, of course I want a second one!"

We both laughed, but I was deadly serious about a second gospel truck to reach more people. At that moment, neither of us had any idea that this was just a small beginning of something that would lead to many more trucks and the winning of many more souls.

We had no idea where this vision would lead us in the near future, but because we agreed and were determined, we got to work on a second gospel truck.

Soon, the same family that sponsored the first truck reached out and provided the money for the second gospel truck. It was so successful that it wouldn't be long before a third truck was built.

In the meantime, the desire grew in our hearts to reach even more people in Tamilnadu with this effective evangelistic tool. When we looked at the facts, we concluded that we could expand our area beyond Uthiramerur, Kanchipuram, the Cheyyur district, and Chengalpattu. We realized that Tamilnadu is much larger, with almost forty districts and over eighty million inhabitants. Our dream was to reach all these precious souls with the message of God's love in Christ Jesus. Therefore, Kingsly organized a conference for Christian leaders in Trichy, a small state in central Tamilnadu.

A YEAR OF EXPANSION

During my next visit, Kingsly organized a conference with a very unique purpose—we would take one truck and share our vision to bring a truck to every district of Tamilnadu. We needed the cooperation of the Body of Christ in every district so that we could reach the millions of precious people in Tamilnadu. We showed we meant business, but many of the pastors and evangelists at the scheduled leaders' conference were quite critical and reserved. You could tell from the looks on their faces what they were thinking. "Are they bragging? Are they for real? Could they really do this? It would cost a million to build forty trucks, right? Could they raise that much money? Could they really keep this great promise?" We promised to take it step by step and that we would trust God for the means to deliver on our promise. And yes, it took a while, but all forty trucks arrived.

In 2018, we started with one truck. That year, we counted almost 20,000 decisions for Christ. In 2019, our truck helped us reach more than 40,000 people who made a choice for Jesus. In 2020, we got a second truck, and the harvest more than doubled to more than 111,000 decisions for Christ. In 2021, we "sowed" our first truck in the Trichy district. That same year, we got more sponsors, and our fleet grew to ten gospel trucks. That year, the harvest increased to almost 400,000 decisions for Jesus.

When will we reach the limit? We didn't know! Yet, 2022 would surprise us the most. It seemed as if God was in a hurry because He sent us a single sponsor who donated over twenty gospel trucks in addition to the twenty we already had, so our fleet grew to forty trucks—our original goal!

A NEW MIRACLE SPONSOR

Let me tell you the story. I happened to read a testimonial from a businessman in the Quote 500 magazine, which featured only multimillionaires. I don't normally read these magazines—most of these multimillionaires simply share how they got rich. These stories were what I call "financial macho testosterone"—typical male talk, bragging about their success. I am not interested in these stories. But then I came across a story of Jim (a pseudonym to protect his identity). Jim's story was different. It was not about money but about Jesus. My attention was immediately captured because his story was so different from the others. Apparently, Jim had a higher purpose in life than making money. He wanted to please God in everything he did.

He was an exception to the rule. Would he be understood in the pool of macho businessmen? He shed light on a world that was extremely rich in money but extremely poor in spirit. He was fishing in a pond that I usually did not fish in.

"How can I encourage Jim in what God called him to do?" I thought.

Jim's family name sounded familiar to me. Suddenly, I realized that Jim had ordered some of my books. When I checked the list of orders, I was indeed surprised to find Jim's name and address. I decided to send Jim an encouraging letter, to let his light shine in the dark world of big money.

After a while, I received a message back from Jim, who was very encouraged by my letter. To my surprise, Jim wrote that he knew about us and our ministry and that he intended to sponsor us. In response, I wrote that I was not after his money, but rather after the precious souls that Jim could possibly reach within the world of big money.

A few months later, I received another email from Jim asking me to check my bank account. To my surprise, Jim had deposited a large donation into my account. To thank him personally, I asked Jim to come over for a cup of coffee. Jim told me that he knew me from his childhood.

"I was about twelve when I first heard you speak, and I've never forgotten it. My grandfather was an elder in that church, and you came to preach." I recognized the names he mentioned and did indeed know his grandfather. What a small world! Jim continued: "When I was growing up, I always wanted to serve God, but I didn't know how. My grandpa said to me, 'Jim, it doesn't matter what you do, if you do it with all your heart for the Lord.'" Jim added, "These wise words gave me the freedom to do something I loved, and I would do it for the Lord. Then I found a product that I liked, and I bought my first item. God spoke to me in an audible voice and said, "Jim, if you are faithful in your work, I will richly bless you!" I had no idea what He meant at the time, but as time went on, my business grew beyond my wildest dreams. That is why I was asked to write in the Quote 500. But really, I am not that interested in money. I just want to please God, and now I can do that by sponsoring His work. When I saw the fruitfulness of what you are doing with the gospel trucks, I felt that I had to invest in your ministry in India!"

Wow. I had never sought Jim out, but in God's mysterious ways, He brought Jim into my life. Since the beginning of that relationship, he has sponsored over twenty trucks, quickly making our vision of a 40-truck fleet a reality. He also sponsored a year-long training program for 250 leaders and evangelists. That year, our harvest grew to over 1.8 million precious souls, although not all forty trucks were fully operational for the entire year, as some were not released until late 2022. In 2023, the harvest continued to grow to nearly three million decisions for Christ. From 2018 to 2023, we have made over five million decisions for Christ. This gigantic harvest exceeded our wildest expectations.

BIG CHALLENGES

In retrospect, we realize that God was in control of all these things. We didn't plan any of this; we were surprised at how God's hand had led us to this great harvest. The sponsors who invested in our work were all God-initiated. I never begged for money, manipulated to give, or forced people to donate. I didn't even seek these sponsors; they sought me out.

> ## GOD IS THE PRINCIPAL, AND I AM THE EXECUTOR. PRINCIPALS PAY THE BILL, AND EXECUTORS DO THE WORK.

If God were to ask Kingsly and I to do even greater things, we would certainly do it, simply because we believe that God would provide the means to do His will and His work. One of my statements is: "God is the principal, and I am the executor. Principals pay the bill, and executors do the work. If the principal does not pay the bill, the executor cannot do the work!" So, it is actually God's problem.

However, we faced and still face great challenges. How would we provide good spiritual food for all these new believers? Where would we get Bibles for them? Where would we find pastors and spiritual fathers to build up and equip these new believers? And where would we get the money to keep our trucks on the road? Each truck would cost us $25,000 per year in operational costs.

And since we have forty trucks, we need a million ($1,000,000) each year just to keep the trucks running, in addition to all the costs of the Bibles and caring for pastors, orphans, widows, lepers, etc.

We are so thankful that we have joined hands with all the pastors across the forty districts. After all, they are the closest to the new converts in their districts. How can we provide them with the resources and help they need to care for the new believers in Christ? Yes, we are faced with challenges that we would have never imagined before, challenges that we feel we cannot ignore and cannot take lightly. So, the only thing we can do and continue to do is look up and ask God to open the windows of heaven again. To remain in perfect peace, I say to myself:

Lord, You are the Master, and I am the servant. I am the one who must do the work. Masters pay the bill while servants do the work. If You pay the bill, I can do the job. I trust You to pay the bill so I can do the job. If You don't pay the bill, I can't do the job. I know I have to wait for Your provision before I can do the job. It's that simple!

This attitude has helped me in a tremendous way to place the burden on the Master and leave it there, so that I can continue to do His work with great joy and pleasure and without stress, because I choose to trust my Heavenly Father. I know He will provide everything I need to fulfill His calling—reach the poor with His good news.

CHAPTER 20
CORONA CRISIS

When the rumor of a contagious virus from China became world news in early 2020, it did not take long for it to spread worldwide.

Because it was front-page news, the mainstream media became the biggest promoter of fear—fear of the spread of the virus. Governments around the world made the most absurd decisions, such as keeping a distance of one and a half meters between individuals, using hand sanitizer, wearing a face mask, registering when visiting a public place, requiring PCR tests, quarantining people who may have been infected for weeks, and placing the elderly in strict isolation, separating them from their children and family, leaving them alone to die without family to comfort them. Anyone who opposed the rules were threatened and fined, and those who refused to be vaccinated were threatened with losing their jobs and income they needed to provide for their family. They imposed curfews and created blanket lockdowns of suspected areas and even entire cities, to name just a few.

The whole world went crazy, and the World Health Organization (WHO) promoted and demanded all these outrageous decisions. Unfortunately, with few exceptions, the whole world blindly followed these untested demands and stuck to them, even though it turned out that none of these things helped at all. Even the double-vaccinated were infected again and again. Even those who had received multiple boosters still got COVID. Worse, as time has shown, many vaccinated people became terminally ill, suffered from epileptic seizures, partial paralysis, and heart failure, and many have even suffered from what they called the "sudden death syndrome"—they simply dropped dead.

CORONA CRISIS

In India, Prime Minister Modi took even worse measures. Overnight, he demanded a total national lockdown, hermetically sealing everything off.

Because tens of millions of rural people were working in the big cities of India, they lost their jobs and income overnight. Where would they go now? No income, no shelter, and their families lived far away in the interior parts of the villages. So, millions and millions rushed to return to their families in their villages. Trains and buses became overloaded, fuller than normal, with people hanging out the sides and on the roofs of the trains and buses. Within a short time, there were no more taxis, buses, or trains available when India went into lockdown. Everything was forced to stand still. Desperate to get back, many started walking with what little they had. They walked with bullock carts, hand trucks, tricycles, tuk-tuks, tractors, and on foot. Most of them walked, carrying their children, their bags, and some food through the scorching heat of the Indian sun, hoping to reach their loved ones in their villages.

However, to prevent the spread of the virus, all state borders were hermetically sealed. So, all these workers trying to go home got stuck at the state borders.

The government quickly set up quarantine camps where these people were locked up in the most horrible conditions. There were no proper hygienic conditions, no food, and no medicine available. There were many reports of fights over food, violence, theft, and rape of women and girls. Diseases broke out, and there was no one to help or care.

To escape this "hell," many people tried to escape unnoticed by avoiding state borders and crossing the jungle to reach their homes. But sometimes, this involved several thousand kilometers of travel.

However, as time went by, we discovered that some had drowned in the rivers because they could not swim. Others traveled through the jungle and were attacked by wild animals or bitten by poisonous snakes. Many simply collapsed from exhaustion and dehydration. Others died of hunger due to lack of food. In fact, many of them died before they ever reached their dream destination: their home and family in their native village. The medicine they gave to "treat" the disease was worse than the disease itself, as more people died from the lockdown than from COVID.

According to researchers, this was by far the largest mass migration in history within the borders of one country. Millions and millions cried out for help, but the government was unable to alleviate the need it had created because of the demand for a total lockdown.

What could we do?

Deeply saddened by the disaster that took place, Sharing Hands offered help. We started raising money to buy food, water, medical supplies, and other aid to give these people hope and bring them home. The government accepted our offer on the condition that all refugees were tested and found to be virus-free. Although we did not agree wholeheartedly, we had no choice but to accept it if we wanted to help these victims. We hired buses and trains to bring them back home and helped them on their journey. Many of these people were so grateful for our help and asked why we were doing it. This was a golden opportunity for us to tell them about Jesus.

Eventually, thousands of them accepted Christ on their way home, and we were also able to pray for their families when we reached their villages. Also, many of their relatives opened their hearts to Jesus Christ. In this way, we were able to help over 50,000 people, and about half of them had accepted Christ as their Savior during this operation.

During our project to help the victims of the corona pandemic, ten of our new gospel trucks were completed and ready to hit the road. So even before they were ever used to preach the gospel, they were used to show our love and God's care for these refugees. We used our trucks to provide them with food, water, and medical care. We showed compassion and kindly asked if we could pray for them. Furthermore, we used our trucks to take them home. We did not have unlimited freedom because of public transportation restrictions, but with our own trucks, we had complete freedom to share the gospel without hindrance.

Since the refugees had no choice but to hear our stories as we brought them to their homes, our heart was to bring them to their true "home"—their eternal destination—by preaching Christ. Many of them had seen our love and compassion and opened their hearts to accept Christ. That made our time and money investment worth the effort because what would have happened if we had not won these precious souls to Christ? After all, didn't we call these trucks "gospel trucks?" Indeed, they fulfilled a higher purpose—to minister to and meet the needs of these "corona victims." Hallelujah!

Even the stumbling block of the corona crisis became a springboard to preach the good news and win more precious people to Christ. Our God has indeed caused "all things" to work together for good to those who love God and are called according to His purpose.

CHAPTER 21

TOUCH THE LEPERS

In addition to people in poverty, India has many lepers. Leprosy is considered a curse in India, and most people are terribly afraid of infection if they come into contact with a leper. For this reason, lepers are absolute outcasts in Indian society: they are shunned, trampled upon, and expelled from society, even though good medical care is available. The infection rate is almost zero if one observes the required hygiene rules.

Nevertheless, many Indians are superstitious and fear the lepers, so they drive them out of their habitat. Many have never received the care they need to lessen their suffering. On the contrary, their bodies are eaten away by this terrible disease, and they slowly waste away and rot. Therefore, they are abandoned and thrown away like manure.

Initially, I had no idea about this problem in India because the West does not have leprosy. Kingsly asked me if I would visit one of the prominent leper camps to encourage and pray for them. I immediately agreed to visit the lepers, although I had no idea what to expect.

On my way to this camp, Kingsly explained that this camp was donated by a famous movie star who later became a politician. Kingsly shared that at one point, this movie star was asked to play the role of Jesus Christ. In order to do this, he started studying the life of Jesus so that he could identify with the role. One of the scenes involved the story of Jesus touching a leper who was then healed. He was so touched by Jesus's compassion and fearlessness of the virus that He did the opposite of what others did. Instead of avoiding lepers, Jesus touched them. Jesus didn't catch the disease; instead, the leper was healed. The story and the heartbeat of Jesus touched this movie star so deeply that he ultimately chose to believe in Jesus.

Because of his fame and enormous fortune, he wanted to do something for the lepers, so he donated part of his wealth to establish this leper camp I was on my way to visit. Inspired by this story, I was determined to touch the lepers, just like Jesus did. I also thought about what else my team and I could do for these poor lepers to help them.

AMBROSE

When we arrived at the center, someone rang a loud bell to call the lepers together. It was customary to call them together in this way for a joint event.

After a few minutes, we saw them coming, one by one, step by step. One man in particular caught my eye. He was a small man, half blind in one eye. His hands and feet were stumps because the disease had eaten away the rest.

He walked and talked vigorously. The disease did not seem to bother him. He stood before the others who were sitting on the ground and spoke to them enthusiastically, encouraging them to put their trust in Jesus, who would make everything right. Then he began to sing with such passion and fervor that it brought tears to my eyes, even though I didn't understand a word he sang. However, it was clear that the hand of God was on this gentle little man. I felt a deep love for this man named Ambrose.

So, we became friends.

After singing, Ambrose and I shared the love of Jesus with the other lepers, and then the team prayed for each one with tender hugs and laying on of hands. Many of them had not been touched or hugged by anyone for years. We distributed food, soap, toothpaste, and blankets. Then we visited those in their huts who were too sick to attend the meeting.

It was extremely painful to see this suffering. Some had become completely blind when the leprosy entered their eyes. Others had lost their arms and legs completely and could only lie down, fully dependent on the help of third parties. It was heartbreaking to see what suffering, what deep loneliness and depression these people dealt with. Moreover, we felt so handicapped because we didn't speak Tamil, and they didn't speak English. Nevertheless, we bathed and embraced them with as much passion as we could.

TOUCH THE LEPERS

As we left the leprosy camp, we all fell silent in the car, processing the suffering we had witnessed, and the feeling of helplessness in our ability to lift the suffering from their shoulders overwhelmed us.

Nevertheless, we were also greatly encouraged by the boldness and faith that Ambrose had expressed in his speech and his songs. Apparently, God was even in the midst of the suffering. Does not our Bible say that He is aware of the pain and suffering of these people, and that He is moved with compassion? Isaiah says:

> *He has no form or comeliness; And when we see Him, There is no beauty that we should desire him. He is despised and rejected by men, A Man of sorrows and acquainted with grief. And we hid, as it were, our faces from Him; He was despised, and we did not esteem him. Surely He has borne our griefs And carried our sorrows; Yet we esteemed Him stricken, Smitten by God, and afflicted. But He was wounded for our transgressions, He was bruised for our iniquities; The chastisement of our peace was upon Him; and by His stripes we are healed. —Isaiah 53:2-5 (NKJV)*

I noticed that many of them had no feet or toes left, only stumps. Many walked barefoot and often stumbled. That's why I provided them all with orthopedic handmade shoes so that they could at least move more easily and safely. So, the plan to do something for these lepers was born.

I looked forward to visiting the leper colony again on my next visit to India with some friends. Ambrosia was excited about our arrival. He encouraged the others in his camp to give us a warm welcome. He called us his special friends from Europe. I felt the same way about Ambrosius and always asked about his well-being. He was still the strong spiritual leader of the lepers, although he was physically weak.

We brought food, soap, toothbrushes, blankets, and lots of hugs and prayers. We saw so much appreciation and gratitude in response to our visit and the little tokens of love we could offer. Ambrosius asked if we could help with the broken water pump. They had no access to clean drinking water. "Can you help us buy a new pump, so we can have clean water again?" I could not say no and immediately said I would take care of it.

Before the team left the leper camp, a friend of mine donated money for the pump. God's provision flowed even before I asked. Thank, you Lord, for your provision!

Due to the COVID restrictions, my last visit to India was in January 2000. In the meantime, the work had grown, even though I could not see it with my own eyes. Many things were under construction in the four years that I could not visit India. It was during my absence that the number of gospel trucks increased to forty. The vision to build a hospital had already been launched, as well as medical centers for lepers. In another chapter, I will share more about the hospital and leprosy clinics.

I planned my next visit to India for January 2024. During my visit at the camp, I missed some of my leper friends who had passed away. Ambrosius, however, was still alive and exuded the same energy as always. However, I noticed how weak he was and that his physical condition was deteriorating. He asked if he could have my sunglasses, as the bright sunlight bothered him. I could not refuse and gladly gave him my sunglasses, which he immediately put on with due pride.

Then he said to me, "I guess you won't see me again! Expect to see me in heaven next time!" Tears filled my eyes as I realized I might not see Ambrosius again on this side of eternity. I prayed with joy once more for my little leper friend before we left the camp. Shortly after my return to the Netherlands, Ambrosius went home to be with his Lord. My love for the lepers was greatly awakened by this little man who was full of Jesus and always had good courage despite his loneliness and suffering.

One time, an old woman with leprosy had a young, healthy girl with her. We asked why a healthy young woman was living with them in the camp. It turned out that she, together with her mother, had been driven out of her village. The fear of leprosy is deeply rooted in Indian society. So sad to think that this healthy, sweet young girl had no choice but to live with her mother in the leprosy camp.

We had the chance to interview the doctor in this camp. He told us that he had lived in the camp for over fourteen years. I asked him about his wife and children. He told us that since he started working in the leper colony, he had been unable to go home. His whole family was controlled by fear and thought he had contracted leprosy. No matter how much he explained that leprosy can only be transmitted through open wounds and that I observe strict hygiene rules to prevent infection, I could convince them otherwise. That's why the doctor had not been home for almost fourteen years.

I was shocked. Imagine all those years without hugs, kisses, or soft touch. No embrace from your children, your wife, your loved ones. He was considered a leper and shared their fate—treated as a danger to society, a curse to the family, and an outcast. How do you survive such emotional anguish? How do you cope with so much unjustified rejection? Even after all these years, he was perfectly healthy and without a trace of leprosy, yet his family continued to cling to the irrational belief that he was a serious threat to be avoided at all costs.

I asked the doctor in disbelief, "How do you deal with your wife's and children's rejection? How do you deal with the sadness that it brings to your life?

He replied, "Well, my joy and comfort come from the hope I bring to these suffering people by healing their wounds. I care for them, I touch them and lift them up, I help and encourage them. Their great gratitude and appreciation comfort me and lift me above my own sorrow and loneliness. I have a new and satisfying purpose in life."

I was stunned and in tears that this doctor had literally given up his life for more than fourteen years to love and care for these "outcasts."

Certainly, these people need our support to do the work of love, to selflessly give our own lives for them. From this meeting, a plan was born to save and improve the lives of these lepers.

During our research, we discovered that India still has a large number of lepers spread throughout the country. Though we had been focused only on the area we had visited, we discovered that there are at least twelve leper villages in the different districts. We wanted to do something to provide at least basic medical care and medicines. Initially, we had no idea what to do, but unexpectedly, help came from an unexpected source while we dreamed about building a hospital in the Uthiramerur district.

CHAPTER 22

RAPHAEL LIFE CARE HOSPITAL

No medical care was available in the Uthiramerur district, where we started our first farm and built our first multi-purpose church.

There was certainly no hospital nearby.

So, we started medical camps on the grounds of our multifunctional church buildings. With the help of a group of doctors and nurses, we set up a medical camp.

All villagers were then invited for a free medical check-up and free medicines. The first nurse did the intake and registered the patients with their name, age, gender, and their physical symptoms, such as pain, itching, bleeding, shortness of breath, etc. The doctor then examined the patient and, if necessary, gave medical advice and a prescription, which he could exchange for the necessary medicines that he sometimes had not received for years at the next doctor. If the problem was really serious, the doctors referred him for a visit to the hospital. Some hospitals offered to help these people for free. However, we had the responsibility to take them there and bring them back. At an average medical camp, which we often held on a Saturday, we could see and help about 200 patients. In total, such a camp costs us 200 to 250 euros. With very little, you can do a lot of good. Hallelujah!

Nevertheless, if there was an acute problem such as a severe hemorrhage during childbirth or an acute inflammation of the appendix, or if someone was bitten by a poisonous snake, the hospital was too far away to get them there in time. On several occasions, patients had died before they reached the hospital to receive medical attention because the government has done nothing to address the most urgent medical needs of the local population.

With all the responsibilities and projects that demanded so much of our time, money, and attention, we didn't really want to take on a new challenge, but we couldn't resist the temptation.

God went before us, and it seemed He was interested even before we launched the plan because we soon found the perfect plot just on the edge of Uthiramerur, the capital. Moreover, it was a piece of land donated by a wealthy Hindu man. He did not know God and had never heard the gospel, but when he contracted COVID, he was rushed to the Christian Medical College Hospital, where he had to fight for his life. He had difficulty breathing and felt like his lungs were leaking. His chances of survival were almost zero. As he struggled to breathe, he sank into a comatose state. There, he had an encounter with Jesus Christ. During that encounter, Jesus said to him, "I will heal you so that you will be a source of blessing to your community!" Indeed, without any human intervention, he came out of his coma a new man, with a completely different outlook on life and a newfound faith in Jesus. After his recovery, he sought ways to become the blessing that Jesus had told him he would be.

With an open mind, he heard about our dream to build a hospital, and because he had been healed in a Christian hospital, he saw building one in his city as a golden opportunity to become a source of blessing to his community. So, he donated his plot of land to us to build it.

> ## IN THAT BELIEF AND TRUST, WE TOOK THE NEXT STEPS ON THE WATER.

We were strengthened in knowing God was involved because of the way we received the land. It was as if Jesus walked on water and said to us, "Come!" So, we stepped out of the boat of natural provision into the waters of supernatural provision. As long as we kept our eyes on Jesus, we would be able to stand against all odds, and we really believed that because we had been given the land in such a supernatural way. We were convinced that He would not give us land to let it lie dormant, but that our God would also provide for the remaining funds to realize the dream of a Christian hospital.

In that belief and trust, we took the next steps on the water. Our friend, who was an architect, brainstormed with us and designed a modern hospital that, once built, would be the most striking and tallest building in the entire region. The plan was fantastic, and the design was great. However, building something so big would certainly cost us a million euros, which we did not have.

So, we needed one more great miracle to make this dream come true. In faith and trust, we took the next step on the water.

Kingsly and I were crazy enough to believe God for the impossible. Without God's intervention, this whole plan would be a disaster, a total flop. If God didn't intervene, we would never be able to realize this dream. But everyone would know that if we did succeed, it would only be because Almighty God intervened on our behalf. And He did! Hallelujah.

MIRACULOUS PROVISION

One of our sponsors had heard about our plan to build a hospital. We had not asked him for money, however, he was moved to act after he read our newsletter where we shared our dream to build the hospital. In his heart, he was convinced he needed to help us.

He asked about our budget, and we told him, reluctantly, that it would cost a million euros to finish the building. We were speechless and astonished when he told us that he would donate the money in full!

After a few weeks, he called us and asked if we could add a ward to treat leprosy patients. To our dismay, we had to tell him that this was impossible in Indian society. The superstition and fear of leprosy would drive everyone away from that hospital. We could only build such clinics near or in the leprosy villages because that would be the only acceptable solution within Indian society. It couldn't even be in the vicinity.

He asked us how many leprosy villages there were in the region. After some research, we learned there were twelve that were in need of a medical clinic.

He then asked how much it would cost to build medical clinics in all twelve villages. We did not know, so we calculated the costs of treating their wounds and providing medication. We discovered that every clinic would cost us about €50,000. With some hesitation, we told our donor the news, and to our surprise and without hesitation, he agreed to donate all twelve leprosy clinics, one by one.

Once again, we were silenced in awe of how God had prospered us beyond our wildest dreams. We had not even thought of leper clinics at first. It was our wonderful sponsor who had a heart for the lepers and wanted them to be admitted to a hospital.

> **WE DREAMED OF IT, BUT WHEN WE WOKE UP, THE REALITY WAS EVEN GREATER THAN OUR DREAM.**

However, since it was impossible to help them through normal channels, he had to creatively find another way to meet their needs. We were overwhelmed by God's love and how He opened the heart of this man, giving him the nerve to do this with us. So, we started building our first leprosy clinic. When it was finished, we reported it to our sponsor. He immediately sent the money to start the second clinic, and so on, until all twelve clinics were built. In the meantime, we had already started building the hospital. Wow, what a miracle; what an amazing miracle of God's goodness! Kingsly and I had dreamed of it, but when we woke up, the reality was even greater than our dream. Blessed be the name of the Lord!

SLOW PROGRESS

As exciting as it was in the beginning, it took longer than expected. We shared the news with our supporters in November 2020, but with COVID still largely dominating, we faced many setbacks and lockdowns for long periods of time. In addition, the paperwork took much longer than expected, partly because of the bureaucracy and because some civil agents expected bribes from us before they would issue their permits. We always refused.

Sometimes, this was frustrating, but we stuck to the vision that God had given us and went on to complete that vision. We did not let anything stop us.

After the hospital shell was in place, we had to wait for government inspection before we could continue with the plastering, plumbing, electrical, and all other matters to complete the work. That would take more than a year. We prayed hard for the green light from the inspectors so that we could finish. Thank God the moment finally arrived for us to go full steam ahead and make the dream come true.

Since the start of this project, we had been thinking about what we would name the hospital. I got the impression to call it Raphael Life Care Hospital.

The word "Rapha" comes from the Hebrew word Yahweh-Rapha, the God who heals. The reason for that name is obvious, as Kingsly and I believe wholeheartedly that Christ is the Healer and that He would be the Master and the heartbeat of this hospital. The doctors and nurses would pray to Him and call upon Him first before they would treat the patients because they believe that He is the best Medicine Man. He is the Healer and the Bringer of Life; He is the One who cares more for the people than anyone else, and He is the heartbeat of this whole project.

All in all, it took more than three years before we could officially open the building in January 2024. Since the COVID restrictions were no longer in force, I visited India with our donor to attend the official opening of the Raphael Life Care Hospital.

This grand opening was a great celebration because it was the fulfillment of a long-cherished dream. We were overwhelmed by strong emotions when we finally saw the building. God's presence was tangible as we entered the lobby and gathered there with all the guests and dignitaries who had been invited.

We sang praises to our God who had made this dream come true. Tears of gratitude flowed freely as we addressed the guests and explained that we believed that God's healing presence as Yahweh-Rapha was the identity of this hospital and that He would do more than just heal sick bodies. We declared that He is the Redeemer, that He would heal even sick souls, sick minds, and sick hearts, and that our patients would receive a touch from the Great Physician, the Lord Jesus Christ!

We prayed and praised God as we toured through every floor and every room in the hospital. Even our big sponsor could not control his emotions and let his tears flow freely. He was speechless when he saw what his investment had done.

However, the hospital had no medical equipment—not even beds, scanners, ventilators, fans, testing machines, or medical supplies. The building would be unable to fulfill its purpose unless we had all these high-tech instruments, and that would be a new challenge for which we would need a miracle—a miracle that would soon happen.

Kingsly requested information to collect high-quality reconditioned machinery and equipment. All together, it would cost us €750,000. This hugely challenged our faith.

During dinner, we shared our dream with a sponsor, but he could only be with us for two days. On the third day, he would leave early for another appointment. Just before he left, he said, "By the way, I feel like I have to pay for all the medical equipment that is needed for the hospital."

Stunned and overwhelmed by this news, it slowly dawned on me that God had answered our prayer before we had even asked. As I am writing this, most of the equipment has been ordered and installed.

By the time you read this book, we expect the hospital will be fully operational and a great source of blessing to all the people of Uthiramerur.

Kingsly and I already have another dream. Beside the hospital was a plot of land. We looked at each other and laughed. It was the perfect place for a medical university that would train locals to become qualified nurses and doctors and meet the needs of the local community.

Kingsly informed me that the owner had already told him he wanted to sell that land to us for a fair price.

I responded, "Let's go there and put our feet on it!"

And so we did. We prayed and lay our dreams and desires before the Lord, who could and would do more than we dared to imagine.

However, that is a story for another time.

CHAPTER 23
NEW CHALLENGES

If you have read all the stories in this book, you cannot fail to notice that the living God has had His hand in all of this. You are now aware of the amazing opportunities, blessings, miracles, supernatural provision and answers, and growth beyond what we had imagined.

But we have also faced enormous challenges.

The ever-increasing need for Bibles, good literature, the training of pastors and leaders to care for these new believers and the funds needed to pay all the bills is a constant concern for us and our team. In addition to all the ongoing projects such as the orphans, widows, lepers, school children, the agricultural project, and the hospital, there are also the costs of publicity and other things. We consider these burdens light compared to the hardships, opposition, hostility, and even persecution we receive. You may have heard the quote, "New levels, new devils!"

We have certainly experienced that in our work, and we still do.

So, it's not all glitz and glory. Just as Paul wrote about his suffering as an apostle in his second epistle to the Corinthians, we, too, have been given our portion. Paul wrote:

Are they servants of Christ? I speak against my senses; I more so: in troubles oftener, in imprisonments oftener, in stripes above measure, in dangers of death often. Five times received I from the Jews forty stripes minus one, three times was I beaten with rods, once was I stoned, three times was I shipwrecked, a day and a day have I spent in the high seas, in journeyings often, in perils of rivers, in perils of robbers, in perils from my own country, in perils from the Gentiles, in perils in the city, in perils in the wilderness, in perils in the sea, in perils among false brethren, in travail and toil, many nights without sleep, in hunger and thirst, many days without food, in cold and nakedness; (and besides these other things, the daily business of providing for all the churches). −2 Corinthians 11:23–28 (author paraphrase)

PERSECUTION

I know the persecution did not just happen to me. Our whole team has experienced their share of heavy opposition and trouble. But they have also experienced God's power and support so that every part of our projects could be realized. I will not compare us to Paul, but we have certainly had our share. On my first trip, I became so ill that many thought I would die. Over the years, we have had to deal with serious opposition, such as religious fanatics who destroyed the extensions of our new churches, stole building materials and expensive tools, and beat up the guards.

On other occasions, they have filed complaints against us, which caused the authorities to turn against us and force us to stop the work. Sometimes, we were threatened with trouble if we did not pay bribes. Worse still, three of our dear pastors were brutally murdered in order to spread fear among us so that we would stop preaching Christ. Financially, banks stopped sending us funds, and only after the donor's serious investigation did the bank release the money, making the excuse that they had lost our documents. Worse still, the government demanded more than half a million euros in deposit for "security reasons." When we refused because we desperately needed those funds to meet the needs of the poor, they revoked our license to receive foreign funds. To make matters worse, they kept more than a hundred thousand euros of our money, even before our license was revoked. Only after a court case were we able to get half of this amount back. To this day, they have been illegally holding this money, money that was meant for the poor.

Recently, one of our team members was seriously interrogated at the airport, treated as an enemy of the state, and sent back without mercy. Shortly after, Kingsly was also severely questioned and intimidated by various officials about all the wonderful work we are doing. They were aware of all our places of residence, names, activities, places we stayed, and our work preaching Christ. They were looking for any faults, shortcomings, legal failures, and violations of the law to justify banning our work. Fortunately, they could not find any reason to bring charges against us. But the hostility and pressure of the enemy is great. The devil is clearly visible in all this opposition.

SUPERNATURAL INTERVENTION

Recently, some members of our Indian gospel truck teams have been facing serious opposition. They were stopped, intimidated, beaten, and threatened with death if they continued. On another occasion, they punctured our tires, broke the windshield, threw the ignition key of the gospel truck into the lake, and beat up our team.

One gospel truck was confiscated, and our team was thrown in jail for several days. We all prayed fervently for them, and then God performed a miracle. After a few days, a high-ranking female police officer visited the police station where our team members were being held. When she investigated the charges against our team, she became enraged at the local police officers. She shouted at them: "What have you done, fools! These are very good people; they do nothing but good. They have committed no crime that deserves this treatment. Release them immediately! And bring the truck back to them—quickly, quickly, quickly! And I want all charges against them burned immediately. Do it now!"

The local policemen quickly and fearfully obeyed their superior officer, and our men were released. We cannot help but think that she was an angel of the Lord—we won't know until eternity.

Nevertheless, we are sure that their release was an answer to our prayers, just an angel released Peter from prison in response to the prayers of the saints. Therefore, we always appreciate your prayers.

When I visited India in January 2024, Kingsly had planned a special meeting with all 225 full-timers. We had our truck teams, drivers, pastors, evangelists, teachers, and medical workers all gathered in one place. Each one of these people is literally on the battlefield day and night, preaching Christ and saving precious souls.

FRIENDS FOREVER

It was very special and emotional to see them all. Many of them I had known for years, men like Vincent, Babu, Moses, Cittibabu, James, David, John, Victor, Jason, Wilson and many others. Over the years, I had come to know them and had experienced their faithfulness, loyalty, friendship, determination, dedication, and love for Christ.

I had seen them do their utmost for His glory. They paid the ultimate price by winning soul after soul, day after day. They stood with their "boots on the ground" every day.

I realized that this was the winning team that God had entrusted to me and Kingsly. I encouraged them and thanked them from the bottom of my heart. Without them, we would never have been able to reap such a great harvest. I commended them for their untiring effort, diligence, and hard work to bring their dear countrymen to life and Christ. "Without these men, we would have never seen such a great harvest!" I said to Kingsly, with tears in my eyes.

I encouraged them to continue with the good work until the trumpet sounds and Christ comes to gather His bride in the clouds.

"We may not meet again on this side of eternity, but let us all remain faithful to our calling and life's mission until the end," I said.

God's presence was great during this meeting. We all lifted our voices to praise our God, and we closed by laying hands on each other to release God's blessings upon them all. Not only did I encourage the others, but they also encouraged me. Only eternity will tell how the divine connection between Kingsly and me could have produced so much fruit and blessing.

And this isn't even the end of the story.
To be continued....

CHAPTER 24

GATHERING OF THE HARVEST

We are definitely living in the last days. It is clear that Christ may come at any time. In light of His soon return, we feel the urgent need to work until He comes, to work until the trumpet sounds, and the dead in Christ shall rise and we will be transformed, and taken up to be with Jesus forever.

When that happens, it will be the most delightful, glorious, and precious day for those who expect God's Son from heaven to deliver us from the wrath to come. Yes, for us, it will be the most glorious and blessed day, and we look forward to it with great excitement and anticipation.

However, the most terrible time on earth that has ever existed will come to those who remain: Seven years of great terror and misery.

The Bible calls this the "Day of the Lord," the "Day of His Vengeance," and the "Day of His Wrath," among many things. It is in light of this coming day that we want to win as many precious human lives as possible for Christ so that they will escape the wrath and join us in heaven.

Our love for God and our fellow human beings is the ultimate driving force behind the work we do—both in the preaching of the gospel but also in the care of widows, orphans, and the poor. It is the same divine flame that God Himself has kindled in our hearts and that has guided us until now.

If you are a born-again believer and know Christ as your Lord and Savior, we invite you to unite your head, hands, and heart with us in this last hour, to win as many of your fellow human beings for Christ as possible, before the trumpet sounds because on that day, it will be too late to provide such wonderful help to those in most need.

Maybe you're not a preacher, teacher, or speaker, but everyone can do something. We can all contribute to building God's house. We can pray, advise, encourage, love, give, or go.

If you can't go yourself, you can go with your gifts, just like Jim did. We hope that our story will ignite or fan the flame of God in your heart and that that flame will burn forever and lead you to fulfill your destiny in Christ.

God bless you.

Kingsly Lazarus and Jaap Dieleman

ABBA CHILD CARE

Abba Child Care is involved in the following projects:

- Evangelism among the unreached
- Gospel truck evangelism
- Medical care for lepers
- Raphael Life Care hospital
- Care for orphans and widows
- Farming God's Way projects
- Clean drinking water supply
- Church planting
- Training Christian leaders
- Sewing lessons for women
- Education for children
- Bible distribution
- First aid in disasters
- Aid to persecuted Christians

You can be involved in our work through your prayers and donations. If you would like to become a partner or donor, please visit www.abbachildcare.org for more information, or contact us for more information at info@abbachildcare.org.

ABOUT THE DE HEILBODE FOUNDATION

After I came to faith in 1977, I desired to preach the gospel. I told everyone everywhere the extraordinary story of my deliverance from the world of drugs and occultism. Magazine articles and radio and television at home and abroad spread my testimony. Through this publicity, many doors were opened to testify of my faith. In 1983, I was officially ordained as a traveling evangelist. Although I became increasingly active in the Netherlands, my heart grew for the unreached in the rest of the world.

I established the De Heilbode Foundation in 1985 to properly manage my missionary work. Since then I have made missionary journeys to almost fifty countries, including Nigeria, Kenya, Uganda, Tanzania, Ghana, India, Indonesia, Thailand, Malaysia, Singapore, Cambodia, Vietnam, China, the Philippines, America, the Antilles, Trinidad, Suriname, the Balkans, Eastern Europe, Lebanon, and most countries in Western Europe.

The goal of De Heilbode was initially to reach the unreached, mainly through evangelistic activities. But that strategy changed over time. Now, I focus mainly on equipping national leaders, workers, and churches through leaders' conferences, revival meetings, and seminars so that they can reach their own countrymen more effectively. In addition to these activities, I also do extensive work for orphans and widows. This work is housed in a separate foundation under the name Abba Child Care International. See our website for more information about this branch of my ministry.

De Heilbode is a faith project made possible by partner donations. If you are interested in this missionary work and would like to stay informed, you can request the digital newsletter.

If you are interested, please send me an email, but if you do not have internet access, please send a postcard to:

Herald of the Good News

Boomkleverlaan 263

3893 JW Zeewolde

E-mail: info@heilbode.nl

Sites:

www.heilbode.nl

www.abbachildcare.org

www.ontzagwekkendnieuwes.nl

www.ingramcontent.com/pod-product-compliance
Lightning Source LLC
Chambersburg PA
CBHW062102080426
42734CB00012B/2729